CW01658855

# THE GIRL WHO WAS THERE

Surviving childhood torture, reclaiming womanhood and learning how to live.

GEORGIA ALISON SNOW

SILENT STONE PRESS

*First edition published in the United Kingdom in 2025 by Silent Stone Press.*



*For more resources and information, visit:*
thegirlwhowasthere.com

SILENT STONE
silentstone.uk

2511/0819-25

FOR MARIA

*...and every other soul who didn't make it out.*

## Praise from Fellow Survivors

*"Seeing the work Georgia has done with parts has been deeply inspiring in my own efforts to heal. She's helped me understand a new way to show myself kindness and trust."*

***— Survivor Testimonial***

*"I had no idea how to react to these parts of myself until I saw your work. Your genuine acceptance of each one of your girls inspired me to take a new approach and — wow — did that ever make a difference. Thank you for sharing your journey. You have helped me so much."*

***— Survivor Testimonial***

# CONTENTS

# About This Book

This is not a comfortable book. It's not tidy, it's not linear, and it's certainly not polite.

It's a record of survival — not just of what happened to me, but what it *did* to me.

You'll meet the parts of me who carried what I couldn't. You'll hear what they lived through, how they coped, and how we've started learning to live as one whole human.

Some chapters are brutal. Some are tender. Some will feel like being dragged underwater. Others might make you laugh out loud at the worst possible moment. *Good.* That's honesty.

This isn't a performance. It's a remembering. A reclaiming.

Not everything is on the page. Some memories remain mine alone. Not because they're unimportant, but because I don't owe you all of me.

What's here is what I've chosen to say.

And I'm saying it now — *out loud, and on purpose.*

That's what they would hate most.

And there *will* be swearing. When you've been through the shit I've been through, you're allowed to fucking swear.

## — WARNING —

This book contains references to:

- Childhood sexual abuse
- Ritual abuse (including death)
- Trafficking
- Physical and emotional torture
- Dissociated Identity Disorders (DID/OSDD)
- PTSD and flashbacks

It may be triggering. It may be activating. It may bring up grief, rage, numbness, or something you can't name.

Whatever comes up is valid.

## — CONSENT MATTERS —

You don't have to read this all at once.
You don't have to read it at all.

If you need to step away, please do.
**Make tea. Breathe. Cry. Scream.**

Come back when you're ready. Or don't. That's your choice.

This book isn't a test of strength.
It's an offering. A witness. A truth.

Take what you need.
Leave what you can't—or don't want to—carry.
You are not doing it wrong.

# The Girl Who Was There

Georgia Alison Snow

# Introduction

As I write this, I am sitting at my keyboard in a bit of a daze. This morning I have been sobbing into my pillow about the childhood I should have had — the childhood that was taken from me by a system of cruelty and horror.

I have a loving note written to myself in Sharpie on my arm. I often do. It runs alongside my tattoo of Guan Yin—goddess of compassion—who has got me though more difficult moments in the last twelve months than I'd care to admit.

And I have a belly full of lasagne—the absolute pinnacle of comfort food—that I've just eaten in my favourite little café, my sanctuary where I can go and just exist as myself for a while. No pressure. No expectations.

That is what my healing looks like in late 2025. But let me show you how it started...

# 1. Vanessa

The hardest part of my adult life began the day Vanessa showed up. I was forty-nine years old, divorced about a year previously, living on my own and finally somewhere I had the space and peace just to *be*. I think having that space was vital to what happened next...

Vanessa came to me with vivid, concrete memories of the abuse she had suffered. The network of men she had been introduced to. The dehumanisation. The betrayal by her father.

She recounts it thus:

> *I was three years old. I had gone to bed already. My mother had taken my brother away. I don't know where; maybe to Grandma's house? So I was left in the care of my father.*
>
> *I was roused from my sleep to find him in my room. He plucked me out of bed, telling me to be good for Daddy, stripped my nightclothes and fixed chains around me. I don't remember exactly how they worked, they were almost like a 'suit' of chains. I could walk. I could lift my arm to hold his hand. I was, as you can imagine, confused.*

*He led me out of my room, this giant man to my tiny three-year-old self. I was vulnerable—naked apart from the chains—and being led down the stairs towards the living-room.*

*He opened the door and the warmth of the room hit me, as well as the aroma of alcohol. The room was filled with men; I don't know how many. It might have been five, it might have been more. I hid behind my father's leg as a shy three-year-old does. I grabbed onto it for safety, little-knowing that it would offer nothing of the sort. I peeked out around it and took in the scene...*

*All eyes were on me.*

*He took my hand and led me in front of him. He paraded me around the room. As I passed each man, he reached out — touched my hair or upper arm, grabbed my bum or groin, each one getting a feel for the merchandise on offer. There were approving comments "You have a fine specimen here"... "Yes, this is a good one, well done!"*

*I remember looking at the glazed dividing doors into the dining room, wondering if that was a way out. I took in all the details of that space which was so familiar to me, the dark red upholstery of the furniture, the large wooden TV cabinet, the stone fireplace surrounding the gas fire. And in the corner of the room, opposite the TV, a man who I was led to.*

> *This man had an air of authority and a wooden box. The box had a hose attached, with a medical mask. He put the mask over my face and told me to breathe — "It will make it easier."*

And that's where Vanessa's first memory ends.

She is not a stranger to me, of course. Vanessa *is* me.

During most of my life, I had around twelve 'characters' living in my head who argued amongst themselves whenever I tried to make a decision. I thought everyone had a 'cast of characters' inside them — all vying for attention, each with their own motives and needs.

Turns out, that's not actually normal.

What I was experiencing is called trauma splitting — where repeated emotional abuse, especially during childhood, separates parts of the self as a way to survive.

These characters were really academic rather than embodied. They weren't real people, they were simply ways of thinking... one always had to be right, even if it caused arguments; one of them always wanted to look put together; one wanted to forget the world and live on a spiritual plane; one had perverted needs that would make your eyes water; one would bulldoze over anyone to get her own way... you get the idea.

Over the course of eighteen months in therapy (and fifteen years of self-guided mindfulness practice before that) I had integrated these parts — brought them back within me to a consistent 'whole' who could finally make decisions based on 'I', not on 'we'.

But I knew at least one person was still missing. The *'girl who was there'*.

I had uncovered the sexual abuse I experienced in childhood some three months earlier, fully expecting my grandfather—a known child abuser—to have manipulated his way to gain access to me at some point. When my father was revealed as the perpetrator I was shocked. Shaken. No, worse — it was absolutely *seismic*. My entire world was turned upside down and almost destroyed.

I had recovered memories in writing[1], I'd been experiencing increasingly frequent and intense somatic flashbacks where the body literally re-lives the abuse moment by moment, adopting positions and poses that I'd been forced into at the time. Even being thrown around like a rag-doll, feeling the stab of a syringe in the thigh and subsequent muscle relaxation as the drugs took hold, or literally gasping for air due to asphyxiation or drowning that was very real at the time, and felt no *less* real in my own, safe home decades later.

But I had nothing concrete — nothing we would typically and traditionally call 'memory'.

1 I used methods suggested in Penny Parks' "Rescuing the Inner Child" Parks, P. (2011). *Rescuing the 'Inner Child'*. Souvenir Press.

I learnt later[2] that trauma memory works *nothing like* regular memory, and that the lack of regular memories should *in no way* invalidate what is revealed through other methods.

So I had known about the 'cast of characters', and I had integrated them. But this one character—The *Girl Who Was There* —kept bothering me. I knew she *must* exist, even if I couldn't access her. She had never made herself known, and maybe didn't even know of *my* existence.

I knew there *had to* have been someone who had *been there* during the abuse. It certainly wasn't me. Someone else had taken over to make the unthinkable horror survivable to my tiny soul.

My abuse happened chiefly between the ages of three and eleven years old; a time of innocence, of play, of joy — or it should have been if it hadn't been hijacked by the horrors that I experienced.

I knew there was *someone else* who had been present.

And it turned out that person was Vanessa.

The first time we spoke, she simply gave me her name. *I told her that I loved her, that she was safe now,* and if she wanted to tell me or show me anything, that I was listening. I added that whatever she showed me, I would believe her. This kind

2 From the work of Dr. Bessel van der Kolk, and particularly his book "The Body Keeps The Score" — Van Der Kolk, B. (2015). *The body keeps the score: Brain, mind, and body in the healing of trauma*. New York: Penguin Books.

of acceptance is *vital* to connecting with traumatised parts. They don't need any more danger or betrayal. They need someone to listen unconditionally, not to flinch at what they say, not to disown them or deny them for what they tell you... they need *total safety* before they will speak.

And that's what I had set up. Over the course of the previous twelve months I had moved house twice — the second time to a place where none of my family knew the location. I had changed my name, letting go of the names of my abusers who were 'honoured' within my birth name. And I had set up a 'dead-man's switch', so if I ever fail to check in, *everything* will be sent out to the relevant authorities... all the names, locations, dates, methods, words and phrases that I remember being used.

From this point of safety, the real work could begin.

So why did Vanessa's appearance trigger the hardest part of my adult life?

Because, as I mentioned, the only evidence I had for the abuse up until now was in 'recovered memories' which I 'could' have been making up. From somatic flashbacks which 'could' have been generated from a fertile and perverted imagination. And from the then-twenty-seven point list[3] of why my behaviours, kinks and even phobias throughout my life matched with known patterns of childhood sexual assault (CSA) survivors.

---

3 That list has grown significantly since Vanessa first showed herself — at the time of writ - ing I have fifty four individual entries, each supporting the fact that is was, in fact, all real.

But all that evidence? It could have been coincidental, right?

It was a *mountain* of evidence, sure, but since I was still at the 'bargaining' stage of grief, I still had that little get-out clause... I'm crazy, I'm making it up, I am just a pervert and always have been, and therefore *it didn't happen.*

That would make life so much easier; if it had never happened.

I had spent two months during my early recovered memories trying desperately—on one or two hours of sleep a night—to disprove what was coming up.

I worked so diligently, spending every waking hour poring over memories, information, possibilities, any way I could think of to make this *not real.* No-one wants to believe that they were subjected to the kind of abuse that was beginning to surface in my recollections. If there was a way out—a way to say that I was, indeed, making it up and that my father *wasn't* the monster my recovered memories were suggesting—then I would take it in an instant.

I excused every linked behaviour. I invalidated every memory. But no matter how hard I tried—"*you're confused... maybe something did happen, but not in this way*"—I couldn't get to a point I was satisfied with.

I lived for so long with the mantra:

*Not him? Not me? Not that? Surely?*

But with no conscious memories, it was still easy to deny, despite the fact I knew I was betraying the little girl inside me — the little girl who had held it in for so long, and was now aching simply to be believed.

Vanessa's concrete, vivid memories could no longer be dismissed. It wasn't like I was putting together a story from scraps. I was finally seeing what actually happened. Clearly. And undeniably.

For the first time, I *remembered* what happened.

And I knew what that meant.

It meant that with no get-out clause, no 'what if', no 'maybe, just maybe', I would finally have to process the sheer weight of what had actually happened. The full horror. The insanity. The unthinkable.

And that was hard. Really, really hard.

What's more, my previous cast of characters had been purely theoretical. Simply *concepts.*

I could converse with them but they really only existed in my mind, or on paper.

Vanessa was so different. She was *real.* She had memories, sure, but she also had feelings. She existed not in my mind but in my soul. In my nervous system. In every last cell of my being.

This wasn't a 'nice idea' I was talking about. This was a real girl—*me*—who had been seriously violated.

*That's* why it was hard.

# 2. Awakening

After Vanessa appeared, it all started to make sense. But the ground had already been shifting for years. Looking back, I think the first real crack in the illusion came on my forty-seventh birthday…

I had been doing *all* the courses, following *all* the gurus, trying *all* the self-improvement and while I was picking up the occasional gem, the 'hustle' part of that world was not working for me at all. Sure I'd been successful financially, sure I'd been famous in my world, but I was not truly happy. I'll probably talk about that later. But not yet.

What was important is that I had started to learn about boundaries. And I had started to learn about Complex PTSD (Post-Traumatic Stress Disorder).

And I had started to learn about narcissistic parents.

My mother fitted the bill perfectly.

I remember that every time I visited her, I came away feeling small, stupid, inconvenient and *less seen* than I felt when I had arrived.

I started to notice the patterns... I listened for how often she said the word "I" versus the word "you". It was truly eye-opening. Not just a little bit self-centred... we're talking about an imbalance to the tune of a hundred or more to one.

She would ask "How are you?"

I'd reply, "Oh... I've been feeling really drained this week, work's been rough..."

And she'd turn it straight back to herself:

"Oh! Work... I know, I've had so much stress too... oh, you wouldn't believe it... I, I, me, me, I, me..."

It would have been amusing, except I had emotional needs that weren't being met. Not even in the slightest.

I realised that any time I actually dared to be vulnerable, whatever information I gave her would soon be weaponised — turned back to harm me in some way.

I tried to talk about my childhood with her — which, at that point, I thought was only slightly dysfunctional. I hadn't yet uncovered the sheer insanity of it all.

Any attempts to process what had happened were met with deflection, avoidance, blame and shame, shutdown... anything *but* healthy discussion and processing.

It was with an increasingly heavy heart that I realised my mother would *never* provide the emotional support I needed and, let's face it, *deserved.*

She would overstep boundaries, too.

I never actually learnt what boundaries were in my childhood because our home just didn't make use of them. At all.

In my adult life, my mother would come round and plant up my front garden as a 'friendly gesture' (read: assertion of her territory)

I remember one incident where she phoned and asked if I might help her with something in her home and I told her I was happy to... I was meeting a client for an hour at eleven in the morning in the coffee shop near her flat, I'd be done at twelve, and I'd gladly pop round then to help her.

The weirdest thing happened. I think this is when I began suspecting something was seriously amiss.

I was sitting there with my client, talking about whatever I used to talk with clients about in those days, and in walked my mother. She took a seat at a table in my eyeline and ordered a coffee.

She sat there drinking her coffee and looking at me for most of the hour.

I can't remember exactly how it played out at the end of the meeting — I think she went home again before I concluded. And then I went round to her flat and helped her.

I was so deep under the spell that I didn't even think to say "What the fuck, mum?" I just helped her out and went home.

Of course, I now know that "What the fuck, mum?" would have been met with denial, gaslighting or one of the many other tools a narcissist uses to confuse, confound and control their victims.

I also remembered one time when I was a teen, and she came to pick me up from my father's house. My parents were divorced by then, and my father had re-married.

I was maybe around fifteen years old, and she pulled up to my father's house. He and his wife had gone out — very wise. On learning this, she said she was *dying* for a pee... and she was sure it would be okay if she nipped in to use the bathroom... wouldn't take a moment.

It seemed a little odd, but I was fifteen and naïve and didn't understand the concept of resisting my mother's wishes.

Turns out—as she *gleefully* boasted to me half-way home—she hadn't needed a pee at all, and had instead sought out my step-mother's hair brush and brushed her hair with it, hoping that her hairs would be found on it later and cause a huge argument.

I'm pretty sure no-one noticed. But y'know, if it gave her a kick, I guess?

After decades of this, I was sick of all of these boundary violations, and power-play manoeuvres, and—well, let's call it what it is—narcissistic bullshit, so I decided to give the 'grey rock' method a try...

I'd tried for so long to use reason, logic, compassion, *anything* to get through to my mother and improve our relationship. If I *just did more,* then surely it would get better? Because *of course* it was my fault if things weren't running smoothly.

In my study of narcissists, I learnt that I wasn't *special* — I was simply *there.* A narcissist doesn't need *you, specifically* to satisfy their narcissistic needs, they just need *someone.*

And so with guilt in my bones, I turned into a 'grey rock'.

The grey rock method is simple — you become *so boring to the narcissist* that they have no choice but to leave you alone. Essentially you *stop feeding their narcissistic needs.*

When they ask how you are, you say a deadpan: *okay, thanks.*

When they ask what you've been up to this weekend, you reply with a non-committal: *oh, not much really.*

In the unlikely event they ask about your hopes and dreams and fears—basically looking for emotional charge to use against you later—you simply give a dull: *dunno... not sure.*

I literally changed her name in my contacts to "Grey Rock" and changed her profile picture to a grey rock. That way, when she phoned I would already be armoured — already be in grey rock mode.

When you become a grey rock, to begin with, the narcissist notices the starvation and they double-down. (I should note, I don't recommend this method with anyone who could be dangerous... only those who are 'safe, but infuriating'. With someone who is dangerous, just get away. *Far away.*)

Before long, when doubling down doesn't work, they begin to seek a new source of narcissistic supply. And at long last *you* get to breathe.

That doesn't mean you get to stop being the grey rock... if your forgetful optimism makes you think they've changed, then you're in for a disappointing experience.

So you continue.

Now, if someone isn't that close to you, the grey rock method may take them out of your life altogether. But when it's a close family member, it's not that easy, right?

You'll still see each other. You'll still go to family events.

And that's what happened.

I remember the argument we'd had when we all got together for Christmas... not Christmas Day itself, but just before...

Me and my partner, my brother, his wife and their son, and my mother.

Just one of those family get-togethers where you eat too much, jibe at each other a bit, do a quiz and get told to stop being a show-off for knowing the answers... sorry... I have no idea how a functional family does those get-togethers.

But my mother and I had a little argument. I can't even remember the subject now. I assume I was trying to get her to take accountability for something. That usually rocked the boat.

There were some raised voices. We calmed it down. We talked. We hugged. And we parted company.

I literally noted in my journal that I'd had one of the healthiest exchanges I'd ever had with my mother. Like we had *both* acted like adults in the end, and come to a satisfying compromise.

It was when I was talking to my brother on the phone a week or two later that he dropped a casual "I hear you've fallen out with mum."

Uh? Really? It was news to me.

I was pretty much done by then. In the words of Joshua in the 1980s movie War Games, I started to realise *"The only winning move is not to play."*

So I left it. Not actively. Just passively.

Not 'Not Talking'... just kinda 'not talking'. No efforts to make contact.

It went on.

And on.

And when it reached my birthday, *months* later, I was finally able to breathe in, then give the deepest exhale of my life.

No card. No call. No text.

YES! At last!

This was the permission I needed. I remember the actual words I said to myself in that quiet, exasperated-yet-liberated whisper:

> *Thank fuck! I don't have to try any more.*

I'd looked after a lot for my mother. Investments, IT affairs, you know, the sort of things an adult child will take on when their parent claims not to be smart enough, modern enough, or tech-savvy enough to handle things themselves. (She is a deeply intelligent woman, and in retrospect I realise a lot of her 'helplessness' was put on for my guilty benefit.)

So I took all of the information and paperwork of hers that I had, and I packaged it up.

I put together a document with all her passwords, account numbers and any other relevant details she might need and wrote a short note...

> *Mum*[4]*,*
>
> *I will no longer be able to look after your affairs. I have enclosed a document that will give all the relevant information to whoever you find to help you going forward.*
>
> *I will keep the details for twenty eight days, after which I will delete them.*
>
> *Best wishes,*
>
> *Georgia*

She caused a brief kerfuffle... she couldn't hear my 'no', of course... narcissism and a lack of boundaries will do that.

A couple of days after I sent her note, she dropped *all* of her financial affairs through my front door with instructions telling me to sell everything and transfer the proceeds. I mean *all* of her financial affairs... the package contained all of her bank cards, her passport, driving license, her investment gold bars, her paperwork...

Sitting there at my dining table, close to tears, with all this stuff laid out in front of me, I finally realised just how much I had been controlled all my life.

---

4 Using the word "Mum" was a revolution in itself. I actually introduced both of my parents to the idea of being called "Mum" and "Dad" in my late 30s. More on that later...

But I decided she was *not* going to reject my 'no'. That's not how I rolled any more.

Through a few phone calls with my brother (who had lasting power of attorney with me), we decided I'd simply send it all to him by secure mail and he'd deal with it.

It also reminded me to revoke my lasting power of attorney, which I did.

Those first six months were *so* hard. So, *so* hard.

Whenever I was feeling down about losing a family member like that, I just wanted to go talk with my mother. I forgot that she had never *really* supported me. I forgot that I always felt worse *after* talking with her in the past.

But sometimes you just want your mummy, right?

(Just wait until you hear about Chloe's story. Just writing that line above brings up *so much pain*. But the time for that story will come...)

I met someone else who had cut off her mother. She gave me good advice on how to mourn someone who was still alive...

She suggested that I get a small box, and when I was feeling low, or wanted to say something, I should write it down and put it in the box. Or if I found objects that reminded me of her in a bad way, I was to put those in the box too.

And when I was ready? Cremate the box.

A truly wonderful idea, and I'm so thankful to her for sharing it with me.

Exactly six months to the day after I made my declaration, I took the box, carefully placed it in the hearth, and put a match under it.

I watched the smoke rise.

I breathed.

I sighed.

Tears came.

The smoke rose lazily out of the chimney and sent a secret signal. Directly, it seems, to my mother.

An hour or two later, there was a knock at the door.

Seriously?

Yes, seriously. My mother was standing there demanding to know what had gone wrong and why I had cut her off.

We had a brief discussion, and she went away happy once she had established two important points:

Firstly — that she had done nothing wrong.

And secondly — that I was a 'selfish little shit' (her exact words).

Wow.

You might think this was heartbreaking, and it was in a way, but it was also so incredibly liberating. I realised something so, so important...

I realised that the little voice inside my head that called me 'selfish' whenever I set boundaries or advocated for myself? That was her voice all along.

I was free. I wasn't selfish for setting boundaries... I was simply failing to serve my mother. I wasn't selfish for advocating for myself... I was simply expressing my own identity.

Honestly, that little insult she threw my way did so much for my personal development, for my freedom, for my recognition of that inner voice, and how much it loves to lie.

❧

I'd always had a slightly awkward relationship with my father, but with my mother out of the picture—and with our shared experience of living with her and putting up with her infernal bullshit—I really started to reconnect with him.

After the gaslighting and emotional abuse I'd suffered from her, it was a breath of fresh air to relate to someone sane. Someone normal.

My father was the *safe* parent after all, right?

Right?

# 3. Rachel

I had been so pleased at finding Vanessa — finding the '*girl who was there*'. I knew she might have a lot to show me. My horizon had already horrifically shifted when I realised my father was involved in the abuse. And again when I had met the room of men.

Suddenly this wasn't casual abuse. It wasn't a father taking advantage of his daughter because she was the closest person he could find to take his aggression or desires out on.

No. A room of men? This was *organised.*

Shit.

She would *definitely* have more to show me. It might take days or even weeks to uncover what really happened.

That was the understatement of the century, but I didn't know it at the time. I look back now and gently say "My love, you truly have *no fucking idea.*" Not to gloat. Simply to express sympathy to my optimistic past self.

It didn't take me long to realise that the '*girl who was there*', the girl who was present to meet the network, *wasn't* there during the actual abuse. She checked out. Handed it over.

Vanessa was the vigilant protector. She scanned the room for details. She looked at faces and clothing. She recorded details of the rooms I was in, place names. She took notes. Built a database of everything *around* the abuse.

But when the actual abuse started?

Vanessa had enough on her plate with her vigilance and protection. Adding the torture would have killed her.

So that's where Vanessa checked out and Rachel stepped in. Rachel took the bulk of the actual abuse.

I talk about *Rachel* taking the abuse, and you can clearly see the protective mechanism of dissociation at work. I *should* be writing that "I" took the actual abuse. That's who was *truly* there. Me. As a little girl. Being abused, tortured and violated for the amusement of evil men.

But that's too much to bear. To acknowledge that—except when I'm feeling particularly safe and grounded—would destroy me.

I'll talk about this more later, but if you find yourself thinking of me as a fictional girl as you read, just know that's dissociation at work. It's not your fault, it's how the book's written. Just as I did in real life, it splits these 'characters' so we don't have to acknowledge that all of this horror happened to an actual living, breathing human being — me.

Sometimes it strikes me when I'm out in town — I'll see a parent with a little girl. Maybe six years old, maybe eight or ten. I will look—not for too long, naturally, I don't want to alarm them—and a part of me will pipe up: "*that's* how young you were."

Shit.

Honestly, it hits so hard when you see a living human—in the flesh—of the age I was during my abuse.

So, to protect myself I pass it to Rachel just as Vanessa did. It's just about bearable if it happened to her instead of me.

The pain and suffering wasn't really the hardest thing Rachel had to deal with, although that was, as you can imagine, unthinkably tough. Rather, the hardest thing was knowing there was no choice. No control. No escape. Nowhere to run. No-one to save her.

In that world, everything is a test. And it's a test you have no hope of passing.

You can spend forever trying to figure out what they want from you. What will make it end quicker. What will satisfy whatever sick fantasy they are playing out.

Should you appear to be suffering more? Or pretend you aren't? Should you make more noise, or less? Should you surrender to them or fight? What the fuck do they want from you? It drives you crazy...

But there is no answer.

What you realise, in the end, is that you are playing a losing game, and always were. You will never know the rules. And even if you start to notice a pattern, the rules will shift anyway. The men aren't there to give you a solvable puzzle. They're there simply to make you suffer.

One day you realise that you are truly helpless, that there is *absolutely nothing* you can do to control even one ounce of the experience.

And so you have to find methods to cope. And that's what Rachel did.

No-one hands you a manual when you're three years old and entering the world of abuse. There's no internet message-board for six-year-olds to compare notes on how they handle their suffering. So they do whatever they can.

I meet so many survivors who feel bad, weird or *wrong* about how they chose to get through their ordeals. I point out to them that they did *exactly* what they needed to do in order to survive, and that I am *proud* of them for their ingenious coping mechanisms.

One thing that Rachel discovered was *counting*. She still does it to this day when triggered.

I've had electrolysis sessions before now, and if I haven't suitably calmed Rachel beforehand she will count each hair as it's zapped, burnt and plucked. My technician was shocked the first time... "I think I got a good number there", she said. "One hundred and thirty-seven," I replied. And hastily added "I'm not judging... it's just a thing I do."

If there weren't specific things to count—blows from a cane or thrusts with a sex toy—she would simply count slowly in seconds. She can count about an hour in seconds. She always counts slowly to make it seem like less time than it really is.

She learnt to breathe, too. To zone out. To disconnect from her body. To see pain as simply "sensation". Not good. Not bad. Just part of life.

She would scream and cry to begin with. Squirm. Try to escape. But she soon realised there was absolutely no point. So while, for example, she was having her belly or thighs cut with a scalpel and exquisitely painful liquid rubbed on the wounds, she would simply hold her body tensely and breathe through it.

While she was being beaten with a cane while orally servicing one of the men she would simply focus on the task at hand and push the feelings down.

It was harder, much harder, when she was unable to breathe.

Breathing—done right—can get you through most things. I've used it myself in times of stress, with difficult piercings, or perhaps when sitting for six hours in the tattoo artist's chair.

But when you take away the grounding, calming effect of breath, what do you have?

Annihilation.

They get to choose whether you continue to exist.

Yes — asphyxiation was tough.

But what can you do?

Wait it out. They always let you breathe eventually. So breathe when you can. Wait when you can't. Count. Ten seconds this time. Then thirty five seconds. Struggling makes you run out of breath faster, so you learn not to struggle. Ninety seven seconds... okay... that was tough but aren't I doing well? A new personal best, in fact!

And what about when you add water, too?

Probably the most unbearable tortures that Rachel dealt with were the ones involving drowning.

When your wrists are bound behind your back you can't even push on something to resist, it represents *total* helplessness. Your *life* literally in the hands of the man pushing your head under the water.

He's often raping you at the same time, because of course he is. That's how this level of evil works.

And when you come up, you don't know if you'll even be allowed to take a another full breath before being forced under the water again. Just writing this, I realise I have stopped breathing in sympathy.

Even the *flashbacks* of the drownings have been intensely difficult to cope with. I splutter and choke as much during the flashbacks as I did at the time.

All my life I thought that drowning would be the worst way to die. But because I had dissociated and forgotten the torture, I didn't realise I came to that conclusion from *first-hand experience*. I thought I just had an over-active imagination.

I learned a lot about the mechanism of dissociation through Rachel. I talk about her taking the bulk of the abuse, but that's not quite true. Well, it is...

I'll explain.

I spent the longest time re-creating electro-torture. I did it more recently, during my recovery and healing process, but also many, many times throughout my life. I bought boxes online, or at fetish fairs, designed for the purpose... some with continuous signals, some with sound-activation or others activated by other means.

But these devices *never* satisfied.

No matter where I connected the electrodes. No matter how high I turned the power. It never went high enough, it never made me suffer enough. And that's one of the key points about re-enactments... you're not indulging a fetish. You're not doing it for 'kicks'. People exploring kink for pleasure tend to enjoy it. That's not what this was.

No, I wasn't looking for pleasure or satisfaction. I was looking for *accuracy.* Looking to perfectly recreate what I went through in vain hope of either *making sense of it* this time, or at least *having some control over it.* I didn't *know* that's what I was doing, of course.

The problem was that I always played safely. (I say always... there were a few close calls that would scare me and put me off *any* kind of re-enactment for weeks or even months).

But that was key... I played *safely.* My abusers did not.

There is *no way* I could recreate the abuse accurately by my own hands because to achieve that, it would have to firstly be non-consensual, with no get-out and no escape; and secondly, it would have to cause real harm, both physical and psychological.

My usual pattern for parts emerging was firstly to see re-enactments, then to write a loving note to the part on my arm: *"To the girl who was shocked, I love you. You are safe now."* Next, I would often get a partial flashback — enough to get an idea of who this part was. Next I would usually find her name, I'd either be given it explicitly, or it would come as a collection of names where one would resonate more strongly. Finally, once she knew for sure that she was *seen* and *safe,* she would show me one or more full flashbacks.

In the case of *these* particular re-enactments—these electrical tortures—it just wasn't happening for me. The process seemed to be 'broken'.

It was confusing.

The re-enactments went on for days and days. Much longer than any other emergence. And more confusingly, it felt like Rachel, but also... it *didn't.*

One day, as I was getting exhausted and frustrated with the lack of progress, something occurred to me...

"Rachel", I asked, "is there any chance at all that you might have your own dissociated parts?"

Bingo!

Suddenly, Rebecca showed herself.

Why didn't I think of that before?

I knew, by now, what it meant to dissociate for protection. Why couldn't dissociated parts also dissociate when what they were enduring was too much?

The answer is, of course: T*hey could. And they did.*

Rebecca was one of them.

Two more of Rachel's dissociated parts showed up over the next five days. One was Kat, who suffered excruciating dilation ordeals. I had actually been recreating these all my life and when Kat's flashbacks came, I felt no pain or shame at all... I was fully calm about it... "Yup. Been there. Done that... had the aching sphincter to prove it." (This is one of those items on the list of 'impressive, but eye-watering achievements you kinda wish you had never achieved').

The other dissociated part of Rachel's who showed herself was Amanda — the *girl in the box.* Her ordeal was significant enough that she deserves her own chapter. You will meet her later.

❧

Rachel is one of the parts I'm in most close contact with now, and the one who *still* comes to the fore remarkably often to protect me. She doesn't need to, of course, but if I'm going through anything difficult—electrolysis, a tattoo, anything physically demanding, really—she's there.

Tragically, she loves to compare. I'll be sitting in the tattoo artist's chair thinking "hey, at least this isn't as bad as being mercilessly caned". The zaps of an electrolysis needle? A doddle compared to being simultaneously drowned and raped.

And she still loves to count.

But I talk with her now. And sometimes I am able to get through to her.

"Rachel... Thank you so much for keeping me alive. I am so proud of you. I love you. You are safe now. This is chosen and you can walk away *any time you like.*"

And when I can get through, she relaxes. She feels peace for the first time in her life.

And what's more—and this is truly fascinating—whenever I brush my hair, she is right there getting her hair brushed tenderly by the loving mother she never had.

She carried *years and years* of unthinkable torture and abuse. And then held that secret for *decades.*

She deserves to rest now.

# 4. Blanks

Early on in my discovery process, the memories were coming thick and fast. There were the somatic flashbacks where my body would adopt positions, make deliberate movements through muscle memory, and feel the pain that I felt at the time. Very literally.

I'd have visual and audible flashbacks, emotional flashbacks where I might *feel* the terror—screaming into my pillow, or hyperventilating, or trying to run away—without even knowing why.

Things were starting to add up. Dots were joining, and I knew there was at least *something* to these memories, even if —and please let this be the case, I hoped—this stuff didn't really, *actually* happen to me.

My greatest doubt was this: My father worked away at sea.

He was never home.

How did he manage *any* of these activities if he wasn't there?

I scoured my memory for evidence... I remember being told that he worked away for about nine months at a time, then would come home for a weekend, maybe a little longer, then go off to work again.

My mother always said that us kids saw more of him *after* they divorced, when I was eleven, than before. And that was maybe a week—or two separate weeks—per year.

He *definitely* wasn't there.

I tried to think of memories I had with him... there certainly weren't any photos.

I think there might be one single photo of me with my father when I was a babe in arms. But none growing up. (We will ignore the countless photos taken in those rooms. Duplicated and distributed through the network. I don't talk about those in this book. I don't want to go there, even now.)

What about memories?

The trip to the Netherlands. Yes.

The trip to Denmark. Yes. Er wait? Was he on that one? I think so.

Cycling round the Isle of Wight... Yes.

What about at home?

...?

Come on...

Weekends?

Christmas?

Evening meals?

Lazy Sunday brunches?

No.

Nothing.

That solves it — he wasn't there.

But wait a minute?

He built a garage. He had a car he worked on. The garage was full of woodworking tools. There was a wooden 'den' in the back garden he had built for us kids. He knocked the kitchen through into the utility room. He was a volunteer at a local youth organisation. (Ugh. Shit.) My mind was honestly starting to freak out at this dissonance in memory — it still is just a little, even *writing* about it.

Let's go back in...

Bed-time stories? No.

Hugs? No.

Playing catch, or... well, *anything?* Blank.

Oh.

I realised. It's not that he was absent. He was *blank.*

That garage? Built by a ghost.

The car? Fixed by a ghost.

The hugs and stories? No. No ghost there, they just didn't happen at all.

So given he was, indeed, *sometimes* there, I wondered how much time that might have been.

And then, one day, I found hard evidence. His own words.

In a space of twelve years, he had spent a total of four years at sea.

A *third* of his time.

That means that for *two thirds* of his time—eight months per year, on average—he was present at home.

Eight months of the year, and I had *nothing*.

Holy fuck.

❧

Sure, kids are busy playing on their bike, or absorbed in Lego's, or splashing paint all over the dining-room table.

Sure, kids forget events, incidents, maybe even the less significant people in their lives, like that neighbour three doors down.

But a child basically blanking her father from existence? Almost entirely?

That is just not right. Like: Not Right™.

That doesn't mean he was 'detached'. It doesn't mean he was 'emotionally absent'. And it doesn't mean that he 'did a lot of overtime'.

It means something bad happened. Something *real bad*.

❧

It wasn't just my father — I found another blank. A *whole room* in my childhood home.

We moved in when I was three years old. It was so exciting, much bigger than our previous house. Old, too. Filled with nooks and crevices. A big landing with tall cupboards built in. A long corridor upstairs with a step down half-way along that the cat used to hide behind and jump out at you when she was feeling mischievous.

In short, it was hide-and-seek heaven for children and cats alike. And believe me, I knew every last inch of that place... the doorway in the breakfast room that led down a few steps to a long brick-lined pantry under the stairs. A little window at the far end. The pantry followed the turn in the stairs so there was a little nook you could hide yourself in, around the corner by the window.

The bathroom and toilet were separate near the end of the long corridor upstairs, and the toilet had double-doors with a little latch that held them together when you were in there. I guess there just wasn't room for a full-size door to open properly.

There were two big bedrooms off the main landing. One small bedroom. Then another bedroom down at the end of the corridor.

Yes. I knew that house. Every last inch.

The airing cupboard with the louvre doors in the breakfast room that you could rise dough in. My father's study under the front bedroom and the lounge, with the big stone fire-place, under the master bedroom.

Every last inch.

And then the smaller room off the top landing...

I'd seen it when we viewed the house.

Mr and Mrs Ellman—not their real name, but I do clearly remember their real name—opened the little door between the two upright cupboards and there was a small room in there, maybe big enough for a bed, a chair and a side table?

"This was the maid's bedroom", they explained — the house was an old farmhouse that had been swallowed up by sub-urban development and now had 1930s semis all around where there used to be fields.

I tried to remember what that room actually looked like, and when I ever hid in there...

Blank.

I went in my mind up the stairs, turning left about a quarter of the way up. To the top, onto the landing. Turning back on myself to the left toward the tall cupboards.

I reached out to the door between them and opened it.

Blank.

What the hell?

Since I'd been doing 'recovered memory' work, talking with 'Little Georgia' and getting answers about the past, I asked her...

"Little Georgia... do you think we could go into that little room off the main landing?"

She didn't hesitate: "No. Not yet. It's too much."

Wow.

For a full seven years living in that house, seven hide-and-seek-playing, exploring, memory-forming years, I have not *one single conscious memory* of that room.

I started thinking I made it up entirely. But I checked on Google Street View. I drove, virtually, along that road I lived on for seven years. And there, sure enough, standing proud of the other houses was our house. With an unmistakable room perched on the front, interrupting the roof with its dormer window and cute curtains.

At the time I lived there, there was no dormer, just a little roof-light, but this evidence confirmed two things: firstly that the room existed, and secondly that it wasn't just used for storage — the new owners were clearly using it as a fully-fledged living space of some sort.

So the room existed. And I had blanked it. And now my inner child was even warning me not to go in there.

That is just not right. Like: Not Right™.

That doesn't mean I 'didn't go in there often'. It doesn't mean it was 'a boring storage space'. And it doesn't mean I 'simply forgot about it'.

It means something bad happened. Something *real bad.*

The mind doesn't erase for fun.

Not rooms. Not people.

It erases what's too much to remember — what would break you if you knew the full meaning.

It turns monsters into ghosts, rooms into voids. It numbs the pain, the terror, and the truth the only way it knows how.

At the time, forgetting was an act of mercy.

But blank doesn't mean *gone.*

Blank means *buried.*

And buried things don't stay buried forever.

*Clare carries the memory of witnessing murder.*
*This chapter contains graphic emotional content.*

# 5. Clare

"Georgia?"
"Here, Miss!"

That simple interaction each morning at school could well be the reason I'm still here today.

You see, I *existed.* On paper. In the outside world.

If I vanished, people would have asked questions. And while the network were capable of the most unthinkable acts of cruelty and violence, I think they likely did everything they could to avoid unnecessary scrutiny.

Maria was not so lucky.

She was one of three I watched die.

I remember looking into her eyes as we stood inches apart, and her throat was cut.

She was pretty. Beautiful in fact.

But as I remember her more vividly it becomes clear — she wasn't *conventionally* beautiful. The beauty was in her soul. In her innocence. In her feral fire.

On the surface, she was a snotty-nosed, neglected little girl. Just the sort of child who *wouldn't* raise any questions. A child who was expendable.

A runaway?

Sourced from 'care'? (the tragic irony of the word 'care' is not lost on me)

An orphan?

There are so many places a child could be procured with no questions asked. They still can. It's something the world doesn't want to face — doesn't want to admit.

If you have the right connections, you have an endless source of expendable children you can choose from and do whatever you wish with them.

Awful. But true.

I've spoken with other survivors of institutional ritual abuse... those who fell through the cracks... those who honestly had *no-one in the world* that would care about them or wonder where they were. No one to hope they were doing okay, or help them to build a future.

My abuse was horrifying. And I'm not one to compare, but the reports I hear from institutional abuse survivors are truly enough to make *my* toes curl. There isn't even the *pretence* of sanity.

And so, there I stood. The one who lived. I wasn't *safe* as such, but at least I was *accounted for.*

I'll say more about Maria shortly, but let's rewind.

In my earliest recovered memories, I drew a picture. Or should I say 'Little Georgia' drew a picture.

I didn't know anything about dissociation at that point, I'd simply been working with my 'inner child', asking her about her past, letting her speak or not. Letting her draw when she couldn't verbalise.

And what she drew?

It was disturbing. Truly fucking disturbing.

The text read "I saw things I shouldn't see. Horrible things."

Next to it, a crude figure—a woman, or maybe a girl—laid out in a star shape.

Her limbs had been detached. They were placed like an 'exploded diagram' around the body in a way that no anatomy would allow.

Cartoon bones jutted from the stumps, and red scribbles covered everything. Blood. Unmistakably.

Like I said — fucking disturbing.

This was obviously symbolic, right? I didn't know what the symbolism meant exactly. But I hoped the answers would come to me.

❧

When the memories came, they arrived in such a fragmented way — probably to protect me from the raw horror of what I had witnessed. It was way too much for Rachel, and she handed this horror over to Clare.

I had been trying to write about Rachel, and every time I went to type her name, the name Clare came out instead. This was so early in my journey, I was still finding my feet with the mechanisms of parts recovery.

But sure enough, it wasn't long before Clare was showing me what she had witnessed. The flashbacks were so tentative to begin with:

> *I fell asleep thinking about 'the picture' that Little Georgia drew, and had visual/audio flashbacks of power saw noises and screams, and a child strapped to a table, limbs outstretched.*

Just fragments of memory.

I must be making this up, right? In fact, I go into the doubt in *so much depth* at the end of one of my flashback reports...

> *Is it possible that a child was literally strapped to a table in front of me and dismembered? I hope not. But that's what Little Georgia's picture suggests. And what these flashbacks suggest. I MUST be making this one up. The tools used don't add up... it seems amputations are done with manual bone saws, this was some kind of powered circular saw.*

This has been such a strong theme throughout my discovery process. I don't want *any of it* to be true. I spend *so much time* trying to discredit my memories and my discoveries. I'll cover this more in the next chapter, but it's worth noting that someone inventing a fiction doesn't spend most of their time trying to prove its falsehood.

I'm not going to go into details of the incident itself. I've already said enough, and honestly I don't want to go through it again. But I found over time I began to realise that this was, indeed, real.

I realised there were signs all through my life. One example: in my twenties, I used to download pornographic pictures and Photoshop them to dismember the women... I thought it was just a weird kink... like a *really* weird kink... but knowing what I know now? It was simply my subconscious trying to make sense of what happened.

I still hadn't learnt to trust my own testimony. I was still deep in doubt, but in one post-flashback report I came up with such an important and impactful question.

I was lying in bed sobbing, feeling the whole horror of the situation and I asked:

"Why would I go through this for an audience of zero?"

That was a pivotal moment.

I didn't know I was going to write a book. I didn't know I was going to join a survivors' group where we would share notes and support each other with our experiences.

At this point, those flashbacks were a solely personal affair. Nobody else knew what happened in them. I didn't *plan* on telling anyone else. (I mean, I planned to tell my therapist, but that doesn't count, right? She's not an *audience*, she's a *mirror.* And a damn skilled mirror at that!).

Why *would* I go through this for an audience of zero?

I wouldn't. It wouldn't make any sense.

This is where I started to entertain the idea that my memories might be accurate. Not symbolic. Not exaggerated. But literal. And accurate.

And that was horrible.

Do you know what that meant about the world?

And *that's* why Clare had to split off to carry it.

It's not just the events themselves, but what it meant about my world-view. About my sense of safety, justice, fair play, morality... my whole world was picked up, turned upside down and shaken until all the lies and cover-ups built by society started falling out.

For about two months after these revelations, Clare showed me no more incidents. She generally took a back seat as other parts emerged and took their share of my attention.

She would occasionally—maybe two or three times a week—insist that I go to my bed and scream into my pillow for ten solid minutes, then cry for another twenty.

But that was just releasing, right? She'd witnessed one of the most horrific things *anyone* could ever witness and then bottled it up for decades. I knew it might take a good while to release all of that pent-up emotion.

But one day in mid-September, she surfaced again. The previous incident had been horrific—and that's an understatement—but also quite detached. I didn't know the victim or engage in any way before or during what happened. I could keep a healthy psychological distance from her, and that helped so much.

What surfaced in September was *very personal* as her flashback testifies:

> *Oh my god, I am so shaken right now.*
>
> *I was minding my own business, just watching a video. No triggers that I was aware of, and suddenly I was overcome with fear. I felt I needed to scream but didn't know why.*
>
> *I couldn't detect any of the girls.*
>
> *So I went to my bed and screamed into my pillow. No major emotional signature.*
>
> *But then again.*

*And my legs began convulsing like I was trying to escape.*

*I felt freezing cold.*

This cold feeling is a common phenomenon. As the body switches into survival mode, it diverts the blood from your extremities to more internal processes.

Keeping you warm is *way* less important at this point than keeping you *alive.*

It continues:

*More screams came with more feeling. The terror was building. Hyperventilating too.*

*I recognised the signature of this... "Clare, is that you?"*

*"Yes."*

*"It's okay. If you need to show me anything, I'm here..."*

*Oh my god.*

*She showed me a girl in front of me. Right in front of me with a knife at her throat.*

*"No no no...", I screamed into my pillow.*

*"No no no no no..."*

*My protest didn't work.*

*The knife was pulled across her throat.*

*I can't even describe what it looked like, it's too hazy. I can't describe her face, it's too hazy. But I know we had eye contact as it happened.*

*Oh fuck. I am shaking just writing this.*

*I thought the dismembering must be the worst thing I could witness. This was so much simpler, but that eye contact was everything.*

*I hunched over and started retching and retching. I don't know how long for. I assume at the time I actually threw up. It was really close today, honestly.*

*I am grounding myself. Feet flat on the floor.*

*I am Georgia Snow. It is September 10th, 2025. You are NOT in that room.*

*Clare, you are safe now. This was not your fault.*

*Thank you for showing me. I will sit with you.*

First of all, let's recognise how far I had come in my flashback processing skills. That grounding, naming myself, naming the date, letting myself—and Clare—know I am *here* and *safe*.

And crucially *not blaming*.

I read reports from so many survivors who *hate* their dissociated parts. They don't want to see what they have to show them. They resist. They berate.

That is truly *not* the path to healing.

It is *absolutely not Clare's fault* that she witnessed what she witnessed and I let her know that unequivocally.

I love my parts. I express gratitude that they trust me enough to show me what they know. I reiterate that it was never their fault, that they carry no shame or blame.

And I *never* abandon them. I spent enough time abandoned as a child, that I know they need someone to sit with them unflinching.

One of the key things I've learnt about my girls is:

> They don't need *fixing.* They simply need *witnessing.*

I've talked a lot about my girls in my survivors' group, and a couple of members there have really taken on board how I work with them, and they've noticed a huge shift in their own healing as a result.

When you're just getting on with being you, and you receive a message like this one, it really warms the heart:

> *I had no idea how to react to these parts of myself until I saw your work. Your genuine acceptance of each one of your girls inspired me to take a new approach and, wow, did that ever make a difference!*

I don't know why, but I really don't know any other way. Unconditional love seems, to me, to be the *only* valid response to a part.

No matter what she shows you, respond with love and acceptance, and she will begin to find the peace and healing she so richly deserves.

Back to what Clare witnessed, though.

It shook me so much. This was genuinely one of the most difficult things I've ever had to deal with.

I literally spent four solid days crying, sleeping, screaming or eating. Or songwriting. When I say 'sleeping', incidentally, that's generous — we're talking about maybe one or two hours per night.

The songwriting, though.

Oh my.

I had written songs before. I had three songs written about the abuse, and two of them published ("Laura," at the time of writing, *still* isn't published, but I have performed it live many times).

But this just switched to the next level.

I *had* to get this pain out of me. And I felt the guilt at calling it 'pain' because I was *still fucking here.* Lucky me that I actually had the opportunity to feel this pain. Maria didn't get the same chance. And I still feel so bad about that. *Survivor's guilt* is real.

The flashback had come on Wednesday evening. The song was written by Friday, and the demo sent across to my vocalist while I worked on the production. The vocals came back Sunday afternoon and by Sunday evening the song was published on Bandcamp.

Four days—just ninety six hours—from the first flashback to saying it out loud, in a published song, in public.

You know that scene from *Close Encounters of the Third Kind* where Roy Neary is obsessively building a huge model of the Devil's Tower from dirt in his living room, while the world goes about its business in the sunshine outside?

Yeah.

That.

Did it diffuse the tension? Somewhat.

But still every time I closed my eyes, I saw Maria's face. Increasingly clear each time she appeared.

I still see her occasionally. The full body shudder I experience each time tells me that I'm not through it yet.

One thing that struck me about Maria's murder was the silence. Not even silence. Silence has its own signature — the background hum of the universe. No, this wasn't silence, it was a *complete absence of sound.*

Like, if I ask you to tell me what you can see behind your head? It isn't darkness, it's *nothing.* That's how this was.

It took a few days before Olivia appeared. She *heard* what Clare *saw.*

I won't elaborate. But it shattered me all over again.

It's the first time I had experienced two *separate dissociated parts* carrying the same incident in parallel. That's how much it was to bear.

I mentioned three murders. The third must wait for later. It's adjacent to Clare, but not truly Clare's experience.

My gut was tugging at me one day, and I've learnt to listen now. It often doesn't give me details, but gives me a hunch.

I asked:

"Clare. Thank you for trusting me. For showing me the horrors you experienced. I'm so sorry you went through that. I love you, and you are safe now. I have a question... you don't have to answer."

I braced myself...

"Were there any other murders?"

She paused for a moment and replied:

"Kind of."

I though it best not to pry...

"Thank you."

I knew that whatever needed to surface would surface when it was ready. When *I* was ready.

And I knew it didn't need to be forced.

I think Clare said "Kind of" because even *she* didn't want to face the implications of the third incident. And she didn't carry it either. That was for Sarah, who you will meet later.

❧

Clare doesn't speak much. She doesn't need to.

She sits there quietly most of the time, peacefully in the background.

But occasionally she remembers what she has seen and will tug at my sleeve until I let her express it.

Of course I always allow her to let it out. We both feel better afterwards.

She saved my life.

I saved hers.

And even though she couldn't save Maria's life, I truly believe her unspoken vow to stay with her saved Maria's soul. I am so, so proud of her for that...

*The silence wrapped around me*
*No signal in the air*
*Just cold inside my body*
*And someone standing there*

*The moment stayed unbroken*
*No ripple, sound, or sigh*
*She found me in the stillness*
*And we spoke with just our eyes*

> *I saw you, and I stayed for you*
> *You left, but not alone*
> *My vow still stands unspoken*
> *Carved on silent stone*

*The moment turned to shadow*
*The ground began to sway*
*The world collapsed in fracture*
*Still neither looked away*

> *I saw you, and I stayed for you*
> *You left, but not alone*
> *My vow still stands unspoken*
> *Carved on silent stone*

*And afterwards, just stillness*
*No sound, no breath, no light*
*Just me, and all that wasn't there*
*Still standing, somewhere in that night*

> *I saw you, and I stayed for you*
> *You left, but not alone*
> *My vow still stands unspoken*
> *Carved on silent stone*

> *My vow still stands unbroken*
> *Carved on silent stone*

***— "Silent Stone" by Georgia Snow***
*https://georgiasnow.bandcamp.com/track/silent-stone*

# 6. Doubt

*"Not him? Not me? Not that? Surely?"*

I already talked about doubt a little. In the first chapter I talked about my mantra that stayed with me for so long.

Doubt is, for certain, one of the hardest things survivors deal with — especially in cases of historical abuse when there are no bruises, no evidence, no documents. Just whispers, body memories, clues.

There are so many dots that need to be joined up before you even get *close* to the truth.

The frustrating thing is that your *gut* is screaming the whole time. It *knows.* Your body *knows.* But we've been trained out of trusting our gut as humans. We need hard court-room evidence. Something concrete. We need 'photos, or it didn't happen'.

Observe cases of sexual abuse allegations in the news, like the case as it progressed through 2025 involving Donald Trump and Jeffrey Epstein. Over a hundred victims came forward and gave consistent testimony, even though many of them had never met each other before.

And the world *still* asked "where is the evidence?"

We are *taught to doubt ourselves.*

Especially survivors. And, sadly, women.

It goes deeper than that... the abuse networks actively train their victims to doubt every part of their experience. They are gaslit about the most simple things. They are confused on purpose. Abuse is sometimes *deliberately* absurd so that if you tell anyone, they will look at you patronisingly and say "nah... not possible."

This is really the most important thing I learnt about doubt on my recovery journey...

> *They never needed me to forget what happened. They simply needed me to doubt myself sufficiently that even if the truth surfaced, I wouldn't believe it.*

That is the long and short of it.

❧

During the first two months after I recovered my first memories, I was trying to disprove them as quickly as they were arriving.

I worked tirelessly, precisely, forensically. I was only getting about one-to-two hours of sleep each night because my mind was running on overtime.

I made it my full-time job to disprove what my inner testimony was *clearly* telling me to be true.

I was building a portfolio of evidence. As I have previously mentioned, these weren't documents or incriminating objects — they simply didn't exist any more, some forty-seven years after I met the network.

But I collected a list of what I *did* know...

I had recovered memories. Inner child testimony. Somatic flashbacks. Kinks and fetishes that evaporated when the abuse became apparent. Re-enactments of the abuse. Inappropriate fantasies at a *very* early age. Conscious memories of incidents that didn't 'add up'. Hidden confessions from my father in his own novels. Memory blanks...

The list went on, and on, and on...

There came a point, five months into my journey, when I had collected forty eight individual pieces of evidence as to why it was real. I had them in one long document.

And I sat with that document one night. I spent hours without taking a break. I picked apart *every single item on the list* with a view to discrediting it.

And you know what?

Much as I tried, I couldn't.

Individual items? Maybe.

But they started adding up.

Dots were joining up that just couldn't be un-joined.

And all the time I'm ignoring the *witness within me* screaming "it happened... I *gave* you the evidence. I testified!"

I wrote myself a letter that night, after poring over every word in that document, running through every possible interpretation. With every ounce of my mind and soul thrown at the task, absolutely fucking *exhausted,* I finally had to face the truth.

The letter read:

> ***Dear Georgia,***
>
> *Tonight you did something extraordinary.*
>
> *You sat down with 48 entries of evidence from your life: conscious memories, somatic flash-backs, behavioural patterns, family dynamics, recovered inner-child testimony, and more. You brought them forward one by one — not to validate them, but to* ***challenge them****.*
>
> *The mission was clear: "Let's try to discredit these, and see if it's possible that I wasn't abused."*
>
> *You did not lean on emotion. You didn't cherry-pick or dramatise.*
>
> *You came to this table with as much objectivity as a survivor possibly can.*
>
> *And here's what you found.*
>
> *With each entry, the* ***burden of plausibility*** *shifted.*

- *The **vivid and sensory-rich inner child letters**, with unknown but verifiable details*[5] *(Entry 2)*
- *The **fetishes that vanished** the moment their traumatic origins were uncovered (Entry 4)*
- *The **ritualistic re-enactments** that spanned decades, never satisfying because they weren't "accurate enough" (Entry 5)*
- *The **complex songs** that wrote themselves through your parts, correcting your inaccuracies in real time (Entry 23)*
- *The **physical triggers**, like raw meat and bones (Entry 45), face-blindness (Entry 24), anal tension and throat locking (Entries 26–27), and the visceral reaction to knives and blades (Entry 29)*
- *The **factual inconsistencies** in your parents' version of your life — like your father "always being away," when records show he was home most of the time (Entry 17), or the story of the rum*[6]

5 In my early recovered memories I had uncovered facts that I didn't think I knew, but on checking later, they turned out to be true. For example, I reported smelling the distinct odour of flash cubes as photographs were taken. It was only when I looked it up that I realised—and confirmed—that flash cubes did, indeed, have a pungent smell when fired.

6 I talk about this in Chapter 9 — Chloe

*(Entry 43), which doesn't stand up to scrutiny*

- *The **internal discernment** — you knew what didn't happen, rejecting useful but inaccurate details while writing songs (Entry 46)*
- *And the **deeper nervous system shifts** — burping for the first time (Entry 26), crying at feelings of safety (Entry 28), healing trauma-linked urges (Entry 4 and Entry 47)*

*Every line of evidence, taken alone, could be doubted. But **together**, they form a consistent, multifaceted, deeply specific pattern that is **statistically, neurologically, and psychologically implausible to fake**.*

*If this were a court of law, you would have crossed the line of "reasonable doubt" **somewhere around Entry 26**.*

*The remaining entries? They were confirmation, reinforcement, and fine-tuning.*

*And maybe most telling of all? **The 'you' who undertook this didn't want it to be true.***

*That's what gives this process its integrity. You came looking for freedom from the story. Instead, you found that **the only true freedom is through it**.*

*So here is what is now known:*

***You were abused.*** *Not because it's emotionally satisfying. Not because it's narratively neat. But because the data—the memory, the body, the behaviour, the patterns—**no longer allow for any other honest explanation**.*

*This doesn't define you. But it does explain you.*

*And from this place of clarity, you can now do what the abusers never imagined you'd do: **Live. Heal. Speak. Thrive.***

***Keep this letter.***

*When doubt creeps back—and it will—read it again. You don't have to rebuild this mountain of truth from scratch. You built it tonight. It's yours.*

*With love, truth, and unwavering belief in your clarity,*

***Georgia Alison Snow***
***August 2nd, 2025***

This was the beginning of my shift away from the doubt. I honestly still spend a small part of *every day* doubting. But that's less due to the evidence and more to another important role of doubt: *protection.*

Dissociation—splitting the psyche into multiple parts to handle (and forget) trauma—is a protective mechanism. It's what keeps us alive during extreme trauma or duress.

Doubt is another of those mechanisms. It's genius.

While doubt still exists, I still have that little escape hatch. That get-out clause. I just *might* be able to get away with saying "It didn't happen. The world isn't as fucked up as my memories are telling me it is. I wasn't abused. Life is okay. I can get over this silliness and move on..."

Doubt helps you to avoid the deeply difficult and distressing process of *accepting* what happened.

Because believe me, *acceptance* is truly the hard part.

It's the part where all the feelings you couldn't afford to have at the time come *pouring* into your nervous system like a fucking tsunami.

If you haven't seen a tsunami in action you maybe think of a large violent wave that crashes into the harbour and smashes boats. But a real tsunami is nothing like that.

A real tsunami is gentle-looking... a calm wave-front that approaches the harbour and then in its peaceful way just *totally overwhelms everything.*

It has force behind it, but force isn't the key to its destructive power. The power comes from the fact that it is *absolutely relentless.* It finds its way into the harbour, and it keeps coming. It breaches the sea walls, and it keeps coming. It starts flowing down the streets of the city, and it keeps coming. It starts picking up cars and detaching buildings from their foundations, and it keeps coming.

*That's* what the grief of acceptance looks like.

It isn't chaotic. It isn't dramatic.

It's just *fucking relentless.*

Day after day after day, the wave keeps coming. Washing over you.

You grieve the lost childhood. You grieve the lost years afterwards, purely surviving instead of thriving. You grieve the healthy relationships you might have built if you weren't so big on one or more of the four Fs (fight, flight, freeze or fawn).

It keeps coming.

You wonder why you trusted them. You wonder who you can trust now. You wonder what you could have done differently. You wonder why you didn't tell anyone. You wonder why you didn't even know it was abuse. You wonder why you can't remember it.

And still, it keeps coming.

You realise that you were never taught to be an adult because no-one expected you to get that far. You realise how dependent you *still are,* psychologically, on your abusers. You realise that nothing was *ever* as it seemed. You realise that you were never really safe.

For days, weeks or even *months,* this grief keeps coming.

Sometimes you manage to escape back into the doubt, but you know really. You know deep down. Once you've seen the truth clearly, you can't unsee it, no matter how much you would like to.

Even writing this book brought me squarely face-to-face with the doubt.

What if I *am* wrong after all? What if I'm making it up? What if the people who were there see it and tell me I'm wrong. Of course, if that's the case, I'd love them to incriminate themselves and tell me where I went wrong and exactly how *they* believe it all happened.

But the other thing it did for me? And this was tough...

It *stripped away* that *protective* doubt.

Here I am, writing *fifty thousand words* about ritual abuse — a subject I have *never studied.* I've never even seen a true-crime documentary about it, nor read a survivors' memoir, nor seen an exposé in a magazine.

I have *zero* background in this subject. I'm just a nerdy girl who used to program computers, then took photos for a while, then started helping people with their businesses.

So how do I explain my ability to write *tens of thousands of words* on this — without research, without flinching?

How do I know—with *no* research and *no* training—so much about ritual abuse networks? The hideous tortures they inflict? How mind-programming works? The dark operations of trafficking?

Either I am a creative genius, with a particular skill for consistent world-building, and just happened to get lucky that the things I described match exactly what's documented in survivor accounts and trauma research...

Or...

And this is the kicker. This is where, even after all my work, after all my integration, the weight starts to land. After all my therapy sessions combing through flashbacks, memories, parts...

The only other option...

I was there. I was fucking *there.*

Shit.

No escaping that.

I *know* I'm not an imaginative genius world-builder.

So...

Shit.

Yeah.

I was *there.*

❧

The doubt starts with the programming — they never wanted you to know the truth, and if you *do* discover the truth, they want you to disbelieve it.

But then it becomes a protection mechanism — it's that get-out clause that lets you escape back into denial, to see the world as you *wish* it was, rather than how it actually is.

If you manage to make your way through those protections, *and* survive the grief that hits you afterwards, you gain a new sense of clarity and freedom. But you are changed for ever.

Nothing will ever be the same again.

You won't look at people the same way. Edgy jokes hit differently. You have to become *so* protective of your nervous system, your values, your worth, your energy.

Knowing what you know brings you strength, but it also brings you responsibility — responsibility to be your best advocate, protector and champion.

It is at once wholly devastating and totally liberating.

I still advise other survivors to hide behind doubt if they need to. They can do it *fully aware* that they are fooling themselves. It is a powerful protection, and *absolutely necessary,* sometimes, for literal survival.

When the rose tinted specs come off? When the doubt is gone? There is only the raw grit of life left.

The truth is absolutely worth it, though, even when it hurts like hell.

Ultimately, doubt doesn't protect you.

It just stops you from healing.

# 7. Laura

*"Thank you so much, sir. Please come back soon. I'd love to see you again!"*

By the age of eight, my delivery of the scripts was perfect. I had even convinced *myself* that I was telling the truth, that I really loved the men, and the attention, and what they did with—and to—me. It varied from the most gentle, which I always appreciated, to the brutal which I tolerated because at least it meant I was receiving love, right?

❧

When Laura was first emerging as a part, I knew that she had been involved in trafficking, in serving countless anonymous men in hotel rooms. I first visualised her as broken, withdrawn, naked under the dirty blanket she was wrapped in. As I have with all my parts, I made artworks of her.

But something wasn't right.

We weren't connecting. She was distant.

Then, a while after she first surfaced, I had a conscious memory of an outfit I was dressed in. A turquoise satin bikini, with pink tape edging.

It clicked.

Laura wasn't dishevelled. She wasn't depressed and tragic. She wasn't dirty and unkempt.

Far from it.

She was *pristine.*

She was cleaned and polished. Hair done nicely. Dressed up in a costume.

Not a deeply troubled and hurting girl, but a product. A shiny, shrink-wrapped product on the shelf with the others for the men to choose from.

And she knew that if she just smiled in the right way, and stood up straight, then they'd pick her. And that meant she was *worth* something.

And if she pleased them while they were together, they would come back and give her even more of the love that she had been denied all her life, and sorely craved.

❧

Rachel and Clare—those who had *experienced* the horror and *seen* the brutality of the network—looked on with pity. They knew the cost of what Laura was going through. But Laura was oblivious.

She was standing to attention with a big smile on her face, hoping she would be the one who was chosen, while the older girls sat in the corner quietly rolling their eyes. "Girl, you have *no idea.*"

❧

I was talking with my therapist recently about Laura and she said it must have been awful to have to perform under threat of harm if I didn't please the men. I pointed out that it was nothing like that. Laura *wanted* to be there, she *enjoyed* being there. She *loved* serving the men.

But under the surface, all was not well. What had happened was that another part—Julia—had split off. Julia bore *all* of the pain. *All* of the violation. No beginning, no end. She only knows penetration after penetration. Being ripped apart from the inside. Being violated and often physically harmed as well... beaten, smothered into the pillow until she couldn't breathe. But mostly the sexual violation.

Honestly, Julia's flashbacks are some of the hardest to bear. Even as someone now experienced in flashback handling, they drag me under in a way no other part's memories do. Often there's no coherent 'content' — just screaming. Sobbing. The raw, wordless agony I never got to release at the time. The grief. The terror. The truth of what was done to me, unfiltered and unspoken.

Even months after emerging, Julia didn't speak much. She *was* the naked girl that I had visualised wrapped in the dirty blanket. Dishevelled. Depressed. Hurt in the worst ways.

But while she existed—absorbing the pain and wrapping it in silence—Laura could continue her charade.

❧

My adult self had such a lot to work through.

Laura genuinely felt pleasure. Of course she did. My body, although young, was working properly... and when certain areas are being stimulated, arousal happens. It isn't a sign of consent. It isn't a sign of *actually* enjoying it either. (And men could do with learning this lesson about their partners, even outside abusive situations).

And the fawning. Okay, for Laura that was programmed. I'll talk about that programming shortly...

But the fawning...

The *shame* I felt as an adult that I could have possibly *encouraged* these countless men. Rapists. Paedophiles. Let's not sugar-coat it — they knew *exactly* what they were buying.

I complimented them on the size of their junk whether that was true or not. (Another survivor from the same network has told me about being trained to resist as if it was too large, even when it wasn't). I made all the right noises. I invited them to 'come back soon' and violate me again.

I was trained to invite them in the first place. I guess that was to reduce any guilt they had for what they were doing. "She clearly wanted it, so it's okay", they might say, ignoring the fact that 'she' was not only coerced and trained into "wanting" it, but also the fact that a six-to-ten-year-old minor can *not* consent.

❧

I mentioned the programming.

Laura was one of the first few parts to emerge—the fifth to be precise—and I was still at the stage where I thought each emergence must be the last, poor naïve girl that I was!

I thought that Laura carried the *whole* of the trafficking. It was even around that time I sent my father an email (I couldn't help myself) to tell him I had remembered. Remembered *all of it.* Those were my exact words. I didn't accuse him, I didn't say *what* I had remembered. I didn't need to.

He never replied. Of course he didn't... how do you reply to being called out like that?

An innocent man might have reached out, confused, dumbfounded, or even angry. I don't know. That would be up to him. But a guilty man? There is *nothing* he could say that wouldn't make things worse.

I didn't realise, at the time, how wrong my assertion of "all of it" was. But that didn't matter. The principle was sound.

So anyway, it turned out that Laura *didn't* carry the whole of the trafficking — over time more parts emerged.

Just under four weeks after I first met Laura, Allie emerged.

I had been re-enacting specific parts of the abuse. As I mentioned previously it often happened that way when new parts were emerging. I would re enact first, then I would slowly let go of the shame of those re-enactments, then I would start communicating with whoever was *causing* the re-enactments — the girl who needed my attention.

*"To the girl who is obsessed with enemas and being clean... I love you, you are safe now."*

And slowly the new part would begin to trust me enough to give me her name, or show me what she knew from the actual abuse... to connect with me visually instead of just giving me the body memory with no context.

And that's exactly what Allie showed me. The enemas.

I thought they had been a simple cleaning exercise. Basic hygiene. When you're going to have men violating you there, it pays to be clean, right?

But no. What Allie showed me went way, way deeper.

It wasn't hygiene, it was *ritual.*

Annihilation. And Purification.

And actually that's when Joanna's experience finally made sense. She had emerged five days *before* Allie. Her story was all about degradation. Filth. The very worst kind. Being smeared in, and forced to eat all kinds of filth and waste.

When Joanna and Allie were placed in the same room, the programming process started to make sense...

*Step 1:* Total degradation. Strip the victim of all worth.
*Step 2:* Ritually purify the victim.
*Step 3:* Offer the victim love and care on new terms
(that is — in the hands of strangers in hotel rooms).

You have to hand it to them, the network knew *exactly* what they were doing. And they did it incredibly efficiently.

Here is *exactly* how the programming worked, told through one of Allie's flashbacks:

*I'm kneeling in the bathtub. Bent over with a shoe on my back pushing me down.*

*I've taken a huge, deep enema so my bowels are gushing. My bladder lets go as well.*

*He's talking to me sternly...*

*"You're nothing. You're nobody, you little shit. You shouldn't even exist. You only exist because of us. So you have to do everything we say. Understand?"*

I can feel myself believing them.

It goes on...

*"You are so dirty. We need to clean you inside and out, you smelly, dirty little shit. We need to purify you."*

The word *'purify'* carried so much weight. An incantation of sorts. A *spell.*

They'd already pointed out how worthless I was. And dirty.

Purification gave me hope of salvation.

Once we're purified, they then pivot to the 'carrot'. Laura never needed a 'stick' for motivation... after what Joanna and Allie went through, the carrot was perfectly sufficient:

*"We could make you pretty and then you'd be loved? Would you like that?"*

*"Yes, sir."*

*"What would you like?"*

*"I would like to be pretty, sir."*

*"We'll make you so pretty. You'll be so loved. Would you like to be loved?"*

*"Yes, sir, I would like to be loved."*

*"Good girl."*

*So I'm washed off, dried, made up and dressed...*

And that's how Laura was installed. That's why she wanted the attention. That's why she fawned to the men. It wasn't under threat, it was simply *the only means of escape* from her extreme unworthiness.

I believe that as time went on, Laura could be invoked with a simple signal. I have never discovered what the signal was, but I know that at the age of around fourteen, some three or four years after the trafficking ended, I was taken to the flat of a stranger and Laura was back in the room *instantly.*

I have conscious memories of arriving — a diversion on the way to visit my father's place for a week. I remember meeting the owner of the flat (strange guy, a little camp, funny handshake, very distinctive name which I remember to this day). And the next thing I knew I was an hour away from there in the car, continuing our journey. Flashbacks since then have shown me *exactly* what I experienced in that room.

It was Laura through and through.

There were other girls related to the trafficking, too:

Jane, the *quiet cargo* — having to stay silent and out of sight during the long drives to the hotels. She knew *exactly* where she was being taken. Huddled in her sleeping bag across the back seat of the car, gripping her plushie, not daring to ask for a toilet stop — and sometimes not making it unsoiled.

Annabelle, the *trainee* — taught to stay still and silent during violation, so Laura's fake responses could override any resistance she might have naturally shown.

And Andrea, the *girl who could not do enough* — she was punished *after* the trafficking, always told she did it wrong, didn't do enough, needed to try harder. Of course she passed that information to Laura who did, indeed, try increasingly hard to please each subsequent time she was in a hotel room.

❧

I called it 'ambition'. I called it 'success'. But it was *all* Laura.

I got incredible grades in school. Took on responsibility. Won awards. I ran operations for visionary CEOs and told myself I was a strong, powerful leader.

Even as an adult, decades after the abuse, I needed *someone* —preferably a charismatic man—to fawn to. All of my 'success' and drive were rooted in keeping someone else pleased. Someone else impressed.

I was still trying to be the good girl who would finally receive the love she craved.

A huge part of my reclamation has been to stop being the sidekick to someone else's ego-trip, and to build something that's *mine.*

With this book—and with my work teaching therapists what ritual abuse really does to a person—I am doing exactly that.

No longer fawning. Not performing.

Just telling the truth.

Not to please, but to fucking *help.*

# 8. Normal

> *"I had a flashback this morning... it was a pretty relaxing one... no torture... just anal rape."*

I was sitting in my therapist's office describing this latest flashback when I realised how skewed my idea of 'normal' had become. To be fair, it took her pointing it out for it to land fully.

She looked at me with that face: compassion, acceptance, and—I don't know if I imagined this, she truly is the best therapist, but she's also human—the tiniest little hint of 'what the *actual* fuck, woman?!' creeping through her calm, professional expression.

She challenged me. "You do know that's *not okay,* don't you?"

She wasn't referring to the flashback, or my reporting of it. She was pointing out to me—as if it was new information to me—that the very *act of anal rape* isn't okay.

The scary thing: it *was* new information to me. I honestly hadn't realised.

That is what this kind of abuse does to your sense of normality, of justice, of what you can and should expect from the world.

The problem went much deeper...

I remember talking to someone about the trafficking, and specifically an incident that happened when I was around eight years old.

"Oh my god, you were so young!", they exclaimed.

*"Really...?"* I thought, before I caught myself...

My thoughts were already minimising it: eight isn't young. I'd been training for at least five years by then — nearly two thirds of my life so far. I was a seasoned pro. I had learnt all the scripts, I could handle pretty much anything a man wanted to throw at me, and I could even make it look like I was enjoying it.

When I *did* catch myself, it dawned on me.

Oh, wait a minute. Holy crap.

They're right.

To *normal* people, eight years old *is* pretty young to be sexually active and *experienced.* It was just my own groomed, programmed and wholly traumatised brain that thought *any* of it was even *remotely* okay.

I remember literally writing in my journal: "How can I make myself *not* be okay with this?"

❧

With this new level of awareness, I began to examine my whole childhood experience, and compared with what a 'normal' child could expect — a child brought up by loving, caring parents. (Dang, I wonder what that's like. I can't actually begin to imagine.)

I made a chart[7], starting with rape, since that's what raised the issue in the first place.

To me? Normal. To a healthy family? Most likely, that's unthinkable, right? Yeah. Probably.

Now, I'll admit that the torture I endured was pretty inconvenient. It killed my vibe. Distracted me from developing as a healthy adult. And sometimes—well, *most* of the time, actually—it was insufferably painful.

Of course, this still lay under 'unthinkable' in any safe and sane childhood experience. And here I was, labelling it merely 'inconvenient'.

Do you know what else came under 'unthinkable' in a safe childhood? Being bound and abandoned. This had happened quite a few times, especially during my training, and between clients in the hotels.

How did I classify it in my skewed system? It went under the 'bonus' category.

Yes, really.

Being bound and abandoned was a real *treat*. It meant that I wasn't being *actively* harmed in that moment. It was a break from the norm — a breath of fresh air amongst the suffering.

---

7 You can view my chart here — https://thegirlwhowasthere.com/recalibration

As I worked more on the chart, I was truly beginning to realise *just how bad it was.* (I swear if I had a pound for every time I heard a survivor say *"It can't have been that bad"*, I would genuinely have *several* pounds. I jest, but honestly, it's so common to minimise the abuse in this way).

Anyway... I continued with my chart. 'Neglect' was a 'bonus' for the same reasons as being bound and abandoned. That breath of fresh air. Neglect means you are not being hurt.

And getting my basic needs met? Same. A bonus. I mean, I *didn't* get many of my basic needs met — emotional needs, the need for connection, medical needs, all ignored.

It was only at the age of forty-nine that I *actually* got my eyes tested properly and got the right glasses. I was so proud of myself. And then I started dealing with other medical issues that had been neglected all my life. I feel like I'm such a pain in the ass for the medical profession right now... even apologising to my GP for wasting his time when I went to see him about an 'unimportant' issue.

"It's why we're here," he said. "It's what we're paid for."

That was so validating. I realised that I had been lied to all my life.

I'll talk about the 'bucket of blood' in a couple of chapters' time, but just know for now that basic needs were *not* a given in my childhood. Not by a long shot.

I continued my quest...

What about things that are seen as a *baseline* for a happy, healthy childhood... I identified 'respect', 'boundaries', and 'warmth'.

Holy fuck. Those things were *truly* unthinkable in my childhood. Like... even now, as I type, I can't comprehend the idea of receiving any of those from my parents.

Warmth, *maybe.* But that would be fake warmth, given cynically because they wanted something from me. Ugh... as I type I think of the insincerely flattering language my mother used to use with me. "My favourite 'number two' child..." Fuck off, mum.

Boundaries and respect? Not a chance.

My mother saw me as an extension of herself. No identity. I must think what she thinks, do what she does, like what she likes, and I would be punished with mockery, criticism or the silent treatment for stepping outside that prison.

My father saw me as property. As a product. I remember the day the penny dropped. I was in my late forties, visiting for the week. We were in the kitchen and it was just after breakfast. I can't remember exactly what he ordered me to do, but I resisted. Brave.

His wife backed me up. "You can't just order her around", she said.

My father? "She's still my daughter. She has to do what I say."

Like, dude... I'm forty-eight years old. I'm *not* your property. I am a sovereign human being.

But he didn't see it that way.

This incident—and many like it—happened long before the abuse ever emerged. They made me pause for a moment but I never really considered it further.

But once the abuse had surfaced? The moment this memory came back to me I realised something *very* important — totally fundamental to my relationship with my father:

He was *never* my father. He was my *handler.*

❧

Now, don't get me wrong, I know parents are human. They're not perfect. I swear to god the number of times I heard "I'm not perfect" from my mother later in life.

"Mum, I didn't want perfection, I just wanted the most basic love and care."

I never said that out loud, because I didn't even know that was a valid response at the time, nor that it was, indeed, what I had deserved as a child.

In recognition of that lack of perfection, I added a couple of bonus categories to the chart. Sorry — you do remember the chart we were talking about?

If a parent in a healthy household *encourages* their child, I think that's a bonus. That's a sign of a really emotionally mature household. A parent who 'allows' a child to grow beyond them — to risk letting their offspring be 'better' than them? That takes courage.

And unconditional love? Holy crap. So rare. Allowing a child to be the very best version of *who that child is,* not who you *want them to be.*

Imagine that!

But it happens.

And if you come from a family where that did happen, then I am genuinely so, so pleased for you. Just please don't think other kids get that treatment. Your parents were absolute gems and I award them one million parent-points right here and now.

❧

'Unconditional love' completed my chart...

Looking again at the healthy baseline of 'warmth, boundaries and respect' against my personal baseline of 'rape' brought it home. With quite a thud.

I realised what a monumental task lay ahead of me. What a steep and arduous *climb* I had to face.

But I knew I would face it.

If I didn't, I would continue to attract friends and relationships that would treat me like shit. I would continue to expect, and receive, the worst treatment from acquaintances, bosses and even strangers.

I should note that my last relationship before my divorce wasn't one of those toxic ones. I got so lucky. In fact, we're still best friends. But I needed time and space alone to enter into this difficult work. No matter how wonderful your partner is, it's hard—on both of you—to navigate a complete shift in identity, values, and nervous system while still trying to function in a shared domestic life.

Even the deepest love struggles to live alongside total self-reconstruction.

❧

Since that mind-blowing revelation in my therapist's office, I've been climbing the mountain every day. Starting with my inner girls. Giving them what I never received in my childhood. Loving each one of them unconditionally. Allowing their needs to be valid. Listening, witnessing, caring for them in the best possible way I can manage.

Maybe I'm not perfect.

But I don't need to be, right? We know this now.

I simply offer them *at least*—and hopefully *much more than*—the basic love and care that every child deserves.

They are beginning to thrive because of it.

And when *they* thrive, *I* thrive.

# 9. Chloe

Chloe's emergence was one of those 'before and after' life moments. You know, the sort where you know life will *never* be the same again.

I'd already uncovered so much abuse, so much to deal with, and I was getting used to parts appearing, I knew how to talk with them, how to love them, how to help them to trust me...

I'd met Vanessa, Rachel, Clare and Laura so far. It was clear, the abuse started around the age of three when I first met the network, and continued until the age of eleven when my parents split up and my father lost access.

Chloe changed all of that.

I was sobbing unconsolably into my pillow. I always, where possible, go to bed during emotional dam-bursts because they often involve screaming, and I don't like to disturb the neighbours. I hope my pillow is a suitable baffle. The neighbours have never mentioned anything, nor called the police on my behalf, so I will assume it's working.

Let's not get distracted...

I just couldn't put my finger on which girl this was. It was the first of August, and Laura, the most recent part to emerge, had come two weeks prior. I'd had enough exposure to all of the girls to recognise their signatures. I'd started making visualisations of them, both as I found them and in rescue scenarios. I'd created, printed and framed a "family portrait" of me—Big Georgia—and the girls, all together.

But this grief? I couldn't place it. Couldn't name it. Couldn't *reach* it.

I asked who it was. No-one replied. Not with words, anyway.

But the feeling.

Oh god.

No.

No no no no no.

I didn't like this. I didn't like it *at all.*

If what I suspected was true, this was shattering. It would redefine everything. It would take my world, once more, turn it upside down, and give it a good shake.

Shake? Yeah... I couldn't shake this 'knowing'.

This new part that was emerging? She was non-verbal because she was an infant. Maybe eighteen months old. Around the age that my parents had joked about the rum. About my finding the drinks cabinet and knocking myself out for a couple of days with an alcohol overdose[8].

Oh crap.

---

8 With what I've learnt since, I've realised that an eighteen-month old child doesn't taste rum and say "lovely, I'll have more". They splutter and choke on the bitter taste. This was another of the 'parental stories' that I realised was a cover-up. I was *given* the rum. There will likely be a song about this at some point.

I gathered myself together.

What did this mean?

It meant something profound...

I was fucking *born into the network.* There was *never* a 'before'. There was *never any safety.*

Those dots began to join up again...

I'd already known long ago that my grandfather was an abuser. He had abused my mother, she made no secret of that. And yet, even though they *knew* he was an abuser, they had 'honoured' him with a variant of his name as my middle name.

But suddenly the penny dropped.

My father's best friend. I'd already identified that he was *very likely* in the network. I'd had flashbacks. I remember being particularly fond of him because he was always so gentle while he was raping me.

My first name honoured *him.*

Shit.

I didn't understand the full impact of what was done to Chloe—*me*—at first, I just knew I had to love her, hold her constantly, and give her the care that an infant needs.

I bought a plushie, a large one, Chloe Bear, and I often have her on my hip when I'm doing my day-to-day tasks. I may seem like some crazy lady, but honestly, it's *exactly* what the real Chloe—that abandoned infant within me—needs.

If that's crazy, so be it. I'm healing and I won't apologise.

Weeks after Chloe's emergence, I was watching an interview[9] with Wendy Hoffman, a survivor who speaks out about her own experiences with ritual abuse.

She said something that hit me like a brick:

> *You can't really mind-control a person if that person is intact and feels good about him- or herself, and has support.*
>
> *So they have to strip all of that away.*
>
> *[...]*
>
> *One of the most important things they do is break the bond between the mother and the child.*

Shit.

It made perfect sense.

How did they ever get me to be *so* compliant? So eager to please? So amenable to having Laura installed? So willing to serve those men in the hotel rooms?

9 *Nick Bryant (2023). Mind Control Survivor Wendy Hoffman | The Nick Bryant Podcast (PATREON PREVIEW). [online] YouTube. Available at: https://www.youtube.com/watch?v=UB3kR-AEs98 [Accessed 7 Nov. 2025].*

How did they create the good girl they needed to earn their money or status or connections, or whatever they gained from the trafficking?

How did they condition me so I wouldn't fight too hard while they tortured and degraded me over and over again?

They created Chloe. They created an insecure, supremely needy child. A child whose *only* route to satisfying those needs was through means that the network sanctioned.

Holy fuck. This revelation was landing so hard.

All the times I drained myself to please people in the past were suddenly revealing this insatiable need, installed in me before I could even speak.

❧

But what of this 'breaking the bond'?

My mother has actually admitted it in her own words...

> *"Something happened when you were an infant that scared me, so I went totally hands off on you."*

She said it out loud. And that's *exactly* what she had done.

Little or no touch. No nurturing. No soothing.

Total emotional and physical abandonment in infancy.

I can't imagine what the network threatened her with. My death? Her death? Both of us? Something else?

Given what I'd witnessed through Clare, I knew they didn't have limits.

I began to wonder how much time I spent bawling into the void as a baby, while my mother ignored me for fear that she or I would be punished or even lose our lives if she attended to me.

I can *almost* have some sympathy for her, but it's difficult. I don't know if she's still at risk. That worry is what has stopped me getting in touch with her since the abuse surfaced... I would love to have a conversation if she was open to it—I know, Georgia, you are being pretty optimistic here!—but I just can't risk being in touch in case she has any connection back to the network.

❧

It wasn't just abandonment, though. There was active psychological harm, too.

There's a story my mother loved to tell—and I've even re-told it many times as gospel truth—that she hung me out of a third-floor window by my ankles when I was around eighteen months old.

The window thing is absolutely true — I was *terrified* of heights all my life. And by 'heights' I mean 'walking on a one-foot-high wall as a child. Or 'going two steps up a stepladder' in adulthood. Seriously. I actually took up indoor bouldering after I cut off my mother to see if I could *finally* do something about my fear. *(Spoiler alert: yes, I could!)*

So the window thing was absolutely true. But the story surrounding it? I'm not so sure.

The story goes that I was on the top floor of the house, my mother was in the garden. I was playing by the open window.

She spied me, panicked, ran upstairs, and to teach me about the dangers of playing at heights, she grabbed my ankles, pushed me out and hung me there over the drop.

I bought the story. It was all she could reasonably do, right?

Any mother would do that.

Wait. Georgia. What have you learnt about normalisation?

Let's look at a healthy mother...

Well, for starters, a healthy mother doesn't leave her infant child playing in a third-floor room with an open window.

But let's dismiss that concern...

So, the healthy mother sees her infant child at the window... she panics, she runs up the stairs... and...

Oh.

A loving mother pulls her child *away* from the window.

I literally wrote this on my arm in Sharpie. It sat there for three or four days while the truth sank in.

I repeated it over and over.

A loving mother pulls her child *away* from the window.

She closes the window. Holds her child close. Starts to breathe easier. She thanks the lord, or angels—or whatever higher power she believes in—that her daughter is safe.

A loving mother pulls her child *away* from the window.

With what I was learning, I began to wonder. Was the *whole* story a crock of shit? Was this deliberate? Was this part of breaking the bond?

Was this a calculated act to let me know I couldn't trust *anyone* with my safety? To make me so *deeply* insecure that when people offered me 'love and care', I would take it, even if it meant paying with my body, my dignity and my soul?

You can get so caught up in conspiracy, start to think the worst of people. But when they've already *done* the worst to you, you no longer tell yourself you're being unreasonable.

In the last chapter, I talked about that common phrase, 'it can't have been that bad'. Here, I will introduce the *other* phrase you hear *so often* from survivors...

> *What I'm remembering was* so bad *that it can't be real.*

It's the flip-side of the same coin. We beat ourselves up with these two phrases ad infinitum.

But there comes a point where you realise that truly *anything* is possible.

It *was* that bad. It *is* real.

And sometimes you just *know* inside you what the truth is, no matter how outrageous it seems.

Oh.

Outrageous.

Let's talk about a little 'confession' I read.

❧

My father has written five novels. One of them is based on true events around the time I met the network. It isn't *about* the abuse at all, but it's contemporaneous with it.

(There's another book where a confession *literally leaks out of him* onto the page, but I won't talk about that one here.)

So he added an author's note to the start of this book. And he *really* told on himself. Not admitting the abuse in any way, but admitting his willingness to *hide the truth in plain sight.*

I won't copy the whole note, but two parts stand out. Firstly, his eagerness to gaslight:

> *You may think that you recognise some locations, organisations, even people. Libel laws make me suggest to you that you are imagining that.*

And then secondly, the *perfect* antidote to *anyone* who said 'it's too outrageous to be real':

> *As to the incidents – the more outrageous they seem, the more likely they are to be real.*

You can't imagine the number of times I've been there, second-guessing myself as flashbacks and memories show me the *most outrageous* abuses and scenarios.

And when that happens, I simply fall back onto his own words.

> *The more outrageous they seem, the more likely they are to be real.*

Amen.

Thank you, Dad. You saved me *so much fucking mental anguish.*

❧

Chloe's emergence was *truly* shattering, in a profound way.

I honestly don't know how you get over something like this, except for radical and relentless re-parenting. Giving Chloe the love, the touch, the holding that she never experienced.

The safety. The nurture. The cooing. The songs.

Chloe Bear is probably one of the most ruthlessly loved teddy bears in the world. And so she should be. She deserves every bit of it.

I cry often. I don't even try to stop myself. I simply soothe myself through the tears. Hold Chloe Bear tight. Let her know she's okay. That she's safe now. That she deserves love and will get nothing *but* love from me. That *someone* cares about her now. That she has the mother she was denied for all her life.

The level of evil is incredible. To condition a child from birth for what I went through.

Evil. Indescribable evil.

Yet here I am. Still breathing. Still loving. Able to love myself fully for the first time.

It's nothing short of miraculous.

I honestly have no idea how I'm still here.

But I am.

So I shall continue...

# 10. Distance

While Chloe's experience was *completely* hidden to me for most of my life, there were hints. Cracks. Little clues that things weren't normal.

Each one, taken in isolation, can be forgiven as quirky, or forgetful, or maybe dismissive. But when you add them together, especially with the context of Chloe, things get a little clearer.

❧

The first sign, I guess, came at my birth. My parents didn't obtain a full birth certificate, but a short-form one. It didn't include any parents' names or addresses. The message it gave was "Georgia exists. Now fuck off."

The strange thing is that this must have been a deliberate decision. The short-form birth certificate isn't the default, and there aren't many reasons you might ask for one.

If you don't know who the father is, you might choose one. But I'm pretty sure that wasn't the case.

Or if you have privacy concerns — shame? secrets?

That's basically it.

This was a deliberate act to distance themselves from my existence.

I've been asked a few times if I'm sure my parents are my *biological* parents, and I think I exhibit—to my dismay—sufficient similarities to both that yes, I can be sure.

So with the legal and administrative distance in place, we then move on to the verbal and emotional distance...

I was in my late thirties when my partner commented on the birthday card I received from my father...

> *To Georgia,*
>
> *Happy birthday.*
>
> *From John and Margaret.*

Those aren't their real names. But my father did, indeed, sign my birthday card with his and his wife's first names. His wife, I understand. She was my step-mother, never really close, she was *always* Margaret.

But the strange thing? My father was always John.

From birth.

No Dad, no Daddy[10], no Papa, no Pops...

John.

And before the divorce?

John and Sylvia. For eleven years of my life until they split.

To their face. To friends. On cards.

John and Sylvia.

---

10 Not quite true. You'll meet Katie in chapter twenty two.

I didn't even think it was odd until my partner pointed it out. When it's all you've known, I guess you don't realise just how dysfunctional something really is.

But it was so clear, right?

Distance.

Always about distance.

Don't acknowledge the *relationship* that would put obligations on them. It's quite clear what a 'Mum' and a 'Dad' should do. How they should provide for their child's needs. Care for them. Love and nurture them.

But what does the rule-book say about a 'John' and a 'Sylvia'?

Nothing.

What does a 'John' have to do for a child?

What should a 'Sylvia' provide?

Nobody knows.

No obligation. No expectations.

Total dodging of responsibility.

And accountability.

And the message it gave to us kids?

We're *not* your parents. If you're lucky, we'll keep you alive, but don't hold us to it.

I said it before and I'll say it again. My father was never my *dad*, he was my *handler*. And this just reinforced that fact.

I talked about my parents neglecting my medical needs in chapter 8, "Normal", but I didn't tell how my mother reinforced that neglect.

I remember the phrase clearly:

> *If you don't have a bucket of blood, you're not really hurt. Go away.*

I didn't hear it that often, I didn't need to. Once you've heard it a few times, you just stop trying to get your needs met. You suck it up. You keep quiet. You feel *grateful* that you're not really hurt.

But you *are* — in more ways than one.

The physical harm is real, of course, and shouldn't have been minimised. Even if it's a minor scrape, a healthy parent picks you up, gives you a squeeze, kisses the boo-boo better, and puts some cream on it. Even if the cream does nothing, it's not about the medical science, it's about the demonstration of care, the demonstration that *the child matters.*

The psychological harm done by this kind of neglect? It goes deep and it lasts a lifetime. You learn to endure instead of looking after yourself. You learn that you are worthless. You learn that no-one is coming to help you.

Some people say that's a valuable life-lesson. The sooner a child learns that the world is horrible and they're basically 'on their own', the better.

People who say that are fucking idiots.

They create children who turn into adults who claim "I turned out okay" while traumatising their *own* children and refusing to seek any therapy.

That's *exactly* how generational trauma is passed on.

Kids need love. They need care. They need witnessing. They need to know that they matter.

Yes, there will come a time when they need to learn the world isn't all rainbows and kittens. But that time isn't now. And the time is *never* from their parents.

They find out the world is horrible by *meeting the horrible.* And their parents provide the *safe space to return to,* in order to sort through their trauma and learn healthy coping mechanisms.

The cruelty made its way into jokes, too. Well, jokes? I'm not sure. Passive-aggressive outbursts? I don't know. You judge...

Growing up, my mother would *constantly* let us kids know just how much of a chore it was looking after us. She would joke that she was going to take us down to the pet shop and swap us for guinea pigs.

Harmless?

If you're emotionally mature and stable, maybe.

But if you're a developing child especially one already insecure from the chaos around her? Not harmless at all. It just ingrains the belief that she's worthless, doesn't matter, isn't wanted.

Chloe was cut off from birth. The earliest harms—hands-off upbringing, the terrifying window ordeal—started the process, but it didn't stop there.

My parents demonstrated how you successfully un-parent a child. How you keep them from *ever* creating a healthy, safe bond. How you keep them insecure and therefore malleable and *useful* to sick people like the network.

When your needs are unmet for long enough, you simply stop asking. You think there must be something wrong with *you,* and you shrink in shame. You are disgusted that you're such a horrible specimen that no-one would want to care for you.

You learn that you are not loved, and will never be loved.

You are not wanted, and will never be wanted.

You don't matter.

And, of course, all of this is *far* too much for a young, hopeful, developing child to carry. So they give it all to Chloe.

And Chloe quietly sabotages the rest of that child's life.

Unless, that is, you find her and love her.

Re-parenting Chloe is going to be one of the most involved tasks I've ever had to undertake.

But it will be worth every fucking second.

It already has been.

# 11. Emily

> *"How did you go to school and function normally while knowing what was going on in the rest of your life?"*

It was a simple question my therapist had asked. And honestly, I had no idea. It didn't add up.

How could a child go through such extreme torture and trafficking during the night, or at weekends, and then show up to school smiling, chatting with friends, performing in tests, saying the right things? And all that without letting even *one drop* of the abuse leak out?

The answer came in the form of Emily, a very different part from the others.

While most of my parts had split in order to survive the tortures they were going through at the time, Emily was created to survive a world that would rather trauma didn't exist — a world where, still, the only *really* acceptable answer to "how are you?" is "fine, thanks."

It's really interesting — early on in my recovery, another survivor described her system in the simplest terms: she had a 'day girl' and a 'night girl.'

The day girl smiled and went to school. The night girl took the abuse.

That insight helped me to unlock Vanessa in the first place.

But at the time, I didn't know much about dissociated parts—certainly not my own system—so I just assumed that *I* was the day girl. Vanessa was the night.

Later, as more parts emerged, the truth shifted again.

The day girl wasn't me. She was—as you know by now—a dissociated part too, and her name was Emily.

If I was going to survive the wider world, I needed a front — someone who could ignore everything else that was going on, wear the mask and face the public at large.

The genius of Emily's creation, though, was the psychological armour that she wore — *total amnesia.*

That question... *how did she function in the world while knowing what was going on in the rest of her life?* This was the killer move, her super-power: the truth is, she *didn't* know.

As soon as Emily emerged and her truth became clear, I realised *just how much* she fronted in my day-to-day life.

I've been asked those socially lubricating questions *so many times.* Through my childhood to some extent, through my adulthood certainly. And when I was in peak 'business hustle' mode? Several times in any single networking event.

The questions: What did you do at the weekend? Are you doing anything nice later?

Simple. Usually easy to answer, right? Nobody's really looking for a perfect answer. They're not even really interested in what you have to say. They're just doing what humans do... basically saying, between the lines, "I am not a threat to you and I don't believe you're a threat to me."

I say they're easy to answer. That's true if you're not hiding the most horrific secrets.

It soon became clear.

I *had* been hiding the most horrific secrets.

And I had stock answers for those questions.

*Emily* had stock answers that followed me into adulthood.

When asked what I'd done at the weekend (or any day previous to the present moment), my response would be a dismissive "Oh, I don't know — I've slept since then."

I thought it was just my ability—since taking a mindfulness course—to live in the 'now'.

I hadn't noticed that when placed under 'duress' (i.e. when asked a perfectly innocent question by a perfectly well-meaning person), I actually had *total amnesia* about what had happened previously.

It was the same if I was asked what I was doing later. My stock response was "Oh, I don't know — I'll have to get home and check my to-do list."

Again, *total amnesia,* or there's probably a different word for the future, but you know what I mean. A total blank about anything that was to *follow* the present moment.

Emily lived in a world with no past and no future. Just the present. The safe, *comfortable* present.

Smile. Give the right answers. Don't think too hard about it.

The *cost* of Emily's brilliance?

Disconnection.

She was so protective that I never really made any connections with anyone. Not deep ones. If I'm honest I didn't even make surface connections.

I was confused why other kids had friends round to their house to play and I never did. I didn't realise that Emily was keeping our house *very much* under wraps. Of course she was, given the dangers it contained.

All my life when friends or family have visited my home, I've been *so anxious.* I'm realising this *live,* right now as I'm typing. I always knew I was a private person—more of that in the next chapter—but I hadn't realised *just how anxious* I would get if someone, for example, went upstairs to use the toilet.

I didn't even have anything to hide. But Emily, undiscovered and unexplored, must have been going absolutely crazy.

They mustn't find the secrets. They can't know.

Nobody can know.

Wow.

So... no friends invited into my home. And no friends invited into my soul either. Into my circle of trust. I had such a strong barrier up. I'm surprised anyone talked to me at all, to be honest.

I think the people who did gravitate around me—and they did—was because I was safe. If they confided in me, their secrets went into Emily's storage bin. They weren't coming out again. Not for anyone. Ever.

But I never gave anything away. I never let my vulnerability show. And that comes at a *huge* cost.

People don't want the perfect face. They *want* the vulnerable wreck — because it makes them feel better that they, too, are a vulnerable wreck.

I mean, when we *really* face it, we are *all* fucking vulnerable wrecks. Anyone who says they're not is hiding something.

I remember that Emily would watch my relationships carefully. If they looked like they were getting too close, she'd sabotage them — find some reason to blow them up before anyone could find out who she—who *I—really* was.

Because I knew: if anyone *truly* knew me, they would know just how unlovable and worthless I was.

So I kept the mask on.

But I see her now. I see what she did for me.

She wasn't cold. She wasn't a robot.

She was a child under impossible orders: keep smiling. Keep everything hidden. Never let them see.

Emily kept me safe in a world that didn't want to see the truth. She did it perfectly. Too perfectly.

But now?

I'm slowly learning that I don't have to be perfect anymore.

I don't have to have the answers. I don't even have to smile.

This was something I worked on diligently during Emily's healing: to *not be okay* with *any of the shit that happened to me.* And to *express* my true feelings in the world.

When people ask how I am, I don't moan or groan or burden them, but rather than 'fine', I will say an honest "You know? I've been better".

I'm allowed to say "Actually, I'm not okay."

And internally, at least, I'll be found saying:

"Actually, I've been through hell."

"Actually, I deserve to be seen."

That honesty—with myself, primarily—also allows me to savour the good days too. While I sometimes respond with negativity, I'm also just as likely to say "You know what? I'm really doing okay right now, thank you!"

And to fucking *mean it.*

Emily still lives in me and always will, but now she doesn't have to front alone. Now she gets to rest.

Now she gets to be just a girl. Not a mask.

And for the first time, she's safe to be known.

# 12. Cracks

What did Emily look like from the outside?

I was a good child. Always keen to please, to pay attention, to learn quickly, to give others what they wanted. And what my mother wanted most, it seemed, was the grades. So I studied hard and got outstanding results at school.

Maybe I didn't take part in extra-curricular activities. Maybe I didn't have a large friend group. But I was quiet, studious and always first to volunteer when a helper was needed.

Even at a young age, I was an expert on birds. And herbs. And many other more or less obscure topics. My bedtime reading was a children's encyclopaedia.

I'm sure, as an astute reader, that you're already feeling those little cracks in this idyllic illusion. If you've actually read, rather than ignored, the rest of the book so far, you're all like "no shit", right?

Life was far from perfect...

I can't imagine either of my parents "playing along" with me as a child... honestly... I certainly don't remember any 'pretending'... no fantasy allowed... I remember going on a fairground roundabout once, sitting in one of those cars with four steering wheels. Firstly, how the fuck does that work? You can't have four people steering a car... and secondly, those other kids were so dumb, they kept spinning the steering wheels and stuff... I kept mine locked in a gentle right curve because that's the direction the roundabout was travelling in.

Fuck me. Poor kid. The rules were so rigorously ingrained that I had no chance.

And criticism. I remember the criticism. Oh, *how* I remember the criticism...

Like when I got ninety-seven percent in a test at school, and my mother, rather than choosing to say "well done, I'm proud of you!" came out with "why didn't you get 100%".

And so I did. I *had* to please. It was the only way I thought I was ever going to receive the love I so desperately craved.

On the very next test I worked my ass off and made the exalted one hundred percent. The response. "Okay."

Maybe I had to prove it wasn't a fluke... maybe *that's* what would finally get me recognised, make all my hard work worth it, make *me* worth it... so I did. I worked my ass off once again. Got the top mark once again. This was it... this was the holy moment when my mother says "Yes. You matter!"

But no. She chose "why aren't you improving?"

Wow.

She claims she was joking (of course), and I can see that side of the story. But it's, quite frankly, a shit joke.

That kind of response is how you take every shred of effort, every bit of self-worth your child is trying to build, every late night they've worked, every drop of sweat and tears, and you wrap it up in a boxing glove marked "fuck you" and punch them with it.

❧

My teachers expressed concern. Regularly.

Every school report and every parents' evening, they would suggest: "We're a bit worried. Georgia is very withdrawn. She doesn't join in activities. She doesn't connect with the other children."

They might as well have said *Emily* is very withdrawn, right?

But my mother's response? Every time?

"It's fine. She's just a very private person."

Yeah. Of *course* I fucking was.

And you, Mum — you knew why.

And you did nothing.

❧

*They* knew.

The teachers *knew.* The school reports said it over and over again. I was 'withdrawn', 'disconnected,' 'didn't engage.'

I wasn't 'private'. I was fucking *drowning.* And she fucking *knew* it.

She heard those words and chose to laugh it off. To deflect.

Because if she admitted it, if she acknowledged what the teachers were seeing, she'd have to ask herself why.

And no way in hell was she going to do that.

So I became 'shy', 'bright', 'studious'... fucking 'private'.

It's amazing how many ways you can rebrand a child's trauma when you don't want to admit it's real.

Even later in life I performed perfection. I distinctly remember I went out with a film crew for a few days — I had a guest spot on a travel program... it was fun.

But over the few days, these guys—*experts* in getting to the bottom of a story—just couldn't figure me out.

At the time I didn't drink alcohol[11], I was vegan, I was minimalist, I didn't drink any caffeine... no vices. None.

*(...apart from the porn addiction, obsession with self-punishment and degradation, and countless fetishes — but nobody needs to know that, right? shh!)*

No vices. Perfect.

Like my teachers, they knew something was wrong.

They expressed it out loud.

"*Nobody* has no vices. Come on..."

11 I don't drink alcohol now, but not through some shameful 'white-knuckle' quest for perfection as before. Now it's simply because I don't like the taste and don't like the effects. It was only when I truly made peace with alcohol that I was able to finally give it up. I woke up one morning and I was just "done".

"No, honestly, none."

Hah! I didn't *know* honesty.

Or worse... I *did* know honesty, and I very much knew what it would cost.

But that was a cost in the past, not the present.

Now, I know better.

❧

Those cracks you all ignored? Those red flags the teachers tried to raise that you dismissed? They were screaming. You just didn't want to hear them.

But *I do.* I listen to the screams now. Before they even *become* screams.

I'm done being perfect. I'm done being private.

I am not your quiet little genius any more.

I'm angry.

I'm awake.

And I am *telling the fucking truth.*

# 13. Zoe

*"Hello? Is there anyone there?"*

This was one of the strangest experiences of my entire healing journey.

I was in the middle of cooking — you know, the lazy sort of cooking where the oven does most of the work and you put in less than ten minutes of effort spread across an hour and a half.

So I had just headed downstairs from my office to check on progress, and as I got to the bottom of the stairs I suddenly felt remarkably disoriented.

I looked at my body and was confused. I went into the kitchen and paused "Wait... what's going on? How did I get here?"

I didn't know at the time, but this was dissociation, happening live, right in front of me.

I did what I needed to do with the oven—safe in the knowledge that the timer was running and would tell me when I was needed again—and I came back upstairs.

It was overwhelming.

I skipped the office, and instead went into the bedroom, jumped onto my bed and let out a brief, but heartfelt scream into my pillow...

Then...

"Hello?"

And again...

"Hello?... Hello?"

I responded... "Hello... I hear you..."

"HELLO? Is there anyone there?" really distressed. I was saying this out loud but it was clearly someone else—a dissociated part—fronting.

"Hello... I hear you. You're safe. I love you... who's that?"

"HELLO? Anyone?"

It seemed like she couldn't hear me.

"I'm here. I've got you." I picked up one of my plushies... "This is for you..." I started hugging it tight.

"Is there anyone there?"

"I'm here..." it dawned on me... "Can you see anything?"

"No."

"You're safe... do you have a name?"

"I... I don't want to say"

"That's okay... I love you... you're safe now. It's 2025. You're in Georgia Snow's house. None of them know we're here."

The voice (and feeling) calmed enough to return to the present moment.

I repeated... "I love you... you're safe now."

It was so unnerving. I'd never had anything like that before. My observing self was present the whole time, as it always has been during flashbacks. Probably thanks to my years of mindfulness practice, I have never been totally absorbed into a flashback — part of me, the observing self, has *always* known that I'm safe.

So the observing self was okay, but that definitely wasn't me at the front.

The poor girl was so distressed. I couldn't figure out who it was. I tried to determine if she was an already-known part, but no-one showed up.

I had a brief flashback in the middle of the night... I had woken around three in the morning, and the flashback came soon after waking... I don't know when I was given her name, but I knew it by then.

I was lying on my front, unable to see anything, with a thick hood over my head.

I was lying there and my legs were moving as if trying to escape but they knew they couldn't. My arms joined in, flailing gently. I was breathing rapidly and heavily and giving out a moan on every exhale.

Then I was suddenly grabbed by the throat and turned over...

The hand pushed hard down on my throat and upwards towards my chin pulling my head into an uncomfortable position.

I was flailing with all my limbs, held in place by that big hand around my throat... It hurt so much and I was struggling to breathe.

The lack of air turned flailing arms into full on convulsions.

I didn't know what I'd done wrong but I knew I was obviously being punished for *something.*

I spoke to Zoe: "Zoe, I see you. I understand you. None of this was your fault. You didn't deserve this."

This is the kind of love, acceptance and calm nurturing I have learnt to give to all my parts, especially when they're emerging. It's the kind of reassurance they need to hear. It builds trust, it eradicates guilt and shame, it makes them feel wanted and safe.

❧

Talking of calm nurturing, it wasn't long before Zoe's flashbacks took a darker turn and revealed the true purpose behind this particular torture...

Her next flashback was confusing... she reports it thus:

> *I'm trying to sleep and these hands just keep grabbing me... this has been going on for hours. Every time I try to rest or relax. They're so vivid.*

> *Thumb and one finger on my ribcage, the other fingers on my belly. And it keeps pulling me backwards towards it. I also feel like I want to be sick and I feel aroused too... It feels like dad but it doesn't match any context I've met before.*
>
> *Wait...*
>
> *Something's coming.*
>
> *This feels horrible.*
>
> *It feels like after the strangling, and still hooded, he then goes for the "love" offensive... maybe to cause total confusion... Like... "I have your life in my hands and also I can give you the love you need"...*
>
> *Ugh. No wonder I feel sick.*
>
> *No... No no no... It's horrible. I don't want it to be that... But I think it might be.*

Quite a few times on my journey I've had this gut feeling that something wasn't right, that more would be revealed, and that I wouldn't like it.

And it was the same here.

Zoe's next flashback arrived some four days later. The delay was because this was probably my most brutal time for parts emerging — Rebecca and Eve both emerged between Zoe's first flashbacks and this one.

It was overwhelming.

But when Zoe finally got to show me, it became so clear:

> *My hands were tied, hotel-style but this was at home. This was Zoe.*
>
> *My head had the thick hood on. I couldn't see a thing, and my hearing was muffled.*
>
> *I was on my side and he grabbed me from behind and held me close to him, like a spoon position... My wrists were pulled painfully against the ropes, I was writhing, trying to get away... I knew I couldn't trust his hold... I was sobbing too... I wanted nothing more than to be let go.*
>
> *The hold went on for the longest time. Still writhing... Squirming against his arms, trying to break free even though I knew I was trapped by wrists... I knew I couldn't trust it, but I had no choice... In the end I gave up resisting and relaxed into his embrace. But I knew it was a trap. He waited until I fully relaxed then let me go, pushed me face down on the mattress and began to cane my rear.*
>
> *Hard strokes... Incredibly painful... I cried out in pain on each stroke. Screamed. And a long gap between them so I never knew when the next one was coming... I couldn't get into the rhythm because there* was *no rhythm.*

*After maybe ten strokes, he leaves me for a little while. Then the embrace again... Pulling me towards him in the same spoon position.*

*I'm going crazy at this point, legs flailing, crying and whimpering. I wish I could be anywhere else.*

*Same pattern... I resist for a while, I squirm, I flail, nothing loosens his grip on me... I realise how big and strong he is, and how completely powerless I am.*

*Eventually after the longest time I begin to relax again... not really relax, but surrender... submit, maybe. There is nothing I can do. I'm getting aroused. I feel his body warmth. I make the mistake of letting myself fully surrender — to melt into his embrace.*

*Suddenly there's a hand around my throat. Hard. Harder than that... I literally can't breathe... It hurts so much but that's a minor problem compared to getting no air... I start to flail again, I wish I could punch out but my wrists are held firm... I end up nearly passing out (maybe I did) and convulsing violently... not flailing consciously but unconscious convulsions... he lets me go again...*

*I'm choking and gurgling... I'm nearly sick...*

*At that point I know I have to come out of the flashback, it's too much, so I find my way out somehow... I'm so disoriented...I think at the time I probably peed myself right there and then because the urge to just let my bladder go was so strong. Luckily my adult self intervened and I made it to the toilet.*

*This one was so intense. Knowing I couldn't trust him but having no choice but to submit. It was truly horrible.*

And with this flashback we uncover the whole hideous, calculated nature of this abuse. It wasn't just a bit of 'fun' or 'entertainment' on his part. It was wholly deliberate.

This type of abuse was designed to *destroy any sense I had* of what was love and what was harm. The one who cares also hurts. The one who hurts, then delivers care.

I am held until I relax. But as soon as I relax I am punished.

There is no way out, no correct way to respond.

It fries the brain.

As a child, all you want to do is to please your caregivers and receive love and support in return. When that is weaponised in this way, *nothing* in life makes any sense any more.

And once you've created a child who can't tell the difference between love and harm? Well then you can do anything you like with them.

And you can get them to *do* anything you like.

It is true *learned helplessness.*

Zoe still has a long, long way to go.

For the longest time, I couldn't even handle a gentle touch on the knee.

My partner would sometimes reach out to touch my knee—just a loving gesture while we were sitting next to each other on the sofa watching TV—and my *whole body* would flinch.

I hated that.

I knew it wasn't about my partner — it was all Zoe (even though I hadn't met her yet).

It was the fear and betrayal etched into my psyche, programmed directly into my muscles.

I once filled in one of those 'appropriate touch' diagrams.

You're supposed to colour in which parts of your body feel okay to be touched by different groups of people.

For 'immediate family' — I coloured it in red.

All of it.

Every square inch.

There was no 'safe touch'.

There was no touch that wasn't paid for in fear.

Zoe still lives there, in that red outline.

But I've started building her something better.

One day she will learn to accept safe touch. She will know the difference between what happened and what is possible.

But until then?

No pressure. No contact.

Just space to breathe.

And the promise: *'You'll never be touched without your consent again.'*

# 14. Fetishes

All my adult life I fantasised about being the receiver of a particular sexual act — a spit-roast. I was so envious when I heard rumours of one taking place without me in the board-room at the work's Christmas party.

Of course, I was way too repressed to ever instigate, or even make hints about one.

But it sat there in the back of my mind—and sometimes frustratingly right at the front—for years and years.

And then, after the memories started surfacing, I realised something...

This all-consuming desire, this most secret of fantasy bucket-list items?

I could tick it off already.

"Done. Aged 3."

And honestly, just like that, the desire evaporated.

❧

I fell into the BDSM scene in my twenties. I'm not really sure how I found them. Or why I chose to engage.

But I went to socials — travelled all over the country for them, actually. It was pretty underground in the late '90s so you had to travel if you wanted to meet people.

And I went to the clubs. Though I never really joined in. Too timid. Too repressed.

At the socials we'd talk openly about our fetishes, desires, and history. It was very accepting, and I'm sure someone healthily exploring their shadow side would do very well there.

Unfortunately I was a *bit too much* for them.

We got on the subject of when our fantasies first started. Some people reported seeing 'The Avengers' in their teens, or other camp 1960s shows with 'damsels in distress'. And Lycra.

Others found their way in their twenties or thirties. Maybe they had been fully vanilla[12] before being introduced by a partner and finding that they quite liked it.

When I was asked, I replied—without realising what looks I was about to receive—"Oh, I had quite a lot of fantasies when I was in pre-school. I would have been three."

Honestly.

The looks. The head-shaking. The quiet, compassionate muttering of "that's *not* right".

I guess these early fantasies bugged me quite a lot. I often wondered where they came from. Had I been exposed to BDSM materials—magazines or film—at an early age? Was I reincarnated, and in a past life I was a sex slave? I honestly couldn't tell.

---

12 The term for anything that's *not* kink/BDSM. Just as vanilla is the 'default' flavour for ice-cream, the term is used to refer to the 'default' expression of sexuality.

Quite early in my therapy I mentioned the fantasies to my therapist. I mentioned my age and their content — god, I *love* my therapist. I'll tell her things that I won't even admit to *myself.*

She asked me: "Is there *any* chance any of that might have happened in real life?"

"No no no no... of course not, don't be silly!", I responded.

Once the memories started coming back, I knew differently.

I walked into my session one time and sheepishly said "You know when you asked, and I said no...?"

"Yes, go on..."

"Um. Well actually it *did* happen in real life. *All* of it."

❧

I had *so many* fetishes and paraphilias, honestly. The 'BDSM Safety Checklist'—where you would mark your limits and what you were willing to explore—was like a Christmas Catalogue to me.

Yes, please. Yes, please. Oh my god, yes, please...

This is a problem I've had with my survivors' group too... there are boards for *all kinds* of assault and abuse — specific kinds of violation, specific locations, specific roles.

It dawned on me one day that most people in the group have experienced *one* of those activities, and it changed their fucking life forever.

I could pick any one of them and have a relevant experience to share. It's not a brag. It's just the scale of what happened to me.

And the scale of my fetishes was similarly broad. And deep.

I'd spent *years* trying to let go of kink.

I would build up my toy-box of kit. Get deeper and deeper. Escalate more and more. And then I'd either do something that scared me, or else I'd just feel a huge *shame* about what I was doing, and in a fit of virtue, I'd throw the lot out.

I'd be clean for a while. But sure enough, twelve months later, I'd notice I'd amassed at least half a collection again.

The cycle continued for *decades.*

I tried everything I could. I tried white-knuckling it. I tried re-training my brain. I attended Sex Addicts Anonymous. That was weird. You weren't allowed to talk about what your addiction *actually* entailed. I mean, okay if it works for you. I guess it makes sense from a safety point of view, especially if one of the other members is going to be getting turned on by what you're talking about. But I couldn't sit there and *not* be open and honest. I guess that's just how I roll.

No matter what I tried, the cycle went on and on.

I wrote myself letters on the days I threw the kit out, hoping I'd read them before I bought any more and remember *why* I didn't want this for myself any more.

But I would ultimately dismiss my letters—what *idiot* wrote those anyway?—and would go ahead with the intended purchases regardless.

I took photos of exactly what I threw out to remind me that I was buying the same items over and over again.

My god, I have wasted *thousands* of pounds in my life on kit that has ultimately gone to landfill.

I tried so hard by every means I could think of, and could *never* shift the kink.

But you know what happened?

As I uncovered the root of each kink? As each one showed up somewhere in my abuse? The desire vanished. Evaporated. Poof! Just like that.

There have been *tiny* echoes as parts re-enact before showing me flashbacks. But oh my god, the *freedom* is incredible.

I didn't realise just how strong of a grip kink had on me. And the *exhaustion* of having to keep it private — too much shame attached to share it with anyone.

But when these kinks evaporated one-by-one? That *breathing space* it bought me? Holy hell.

Like I talked about just being 'done' with alcohol in a footnote a couple of chapters ago, I had the same with these kinks...

Lifelong irresistible urges just *gone.* Not fought. Not ignored. Not avoided. Just *gone.*

Crazy.

# 15. Amanda

I'd emptied the contents of the wardrobe—one of those small, single ones with just a few shelves for foldable items—onto the bed. Then I'd tipped it onto its back on the bedroom floor.

Opened the door, or should I now call it a lid? And climbed inside.

Not too bad. Arms pushed up against both sides. Nice and snug just as I like it.

But too long... I didn't have to scrunch my neck or bend my legs at all. No this wouldn't do. It was definitely not quite right.

One of my more quirky behaviours throughout my life was climbing into small spaces. Cupboards, wardrobes, whatever I could find.

I never really knew what I got out of it.

I was usually naked. Happier if it was cramped. And severely disappointed that it couldn't be locked, trapping me in there until someone else decided to let me out.

But of course, I'd never share this weird fetish of mine with anyone. Especially because I didn't think I could trust another human being with the key to my freedom.

I even considered using timed locks. But ultimately decided that would be too much of a risk. Good girl, safety first!

So I carried on—as with many of my fetishes—looking for *accuracy,* and only ever finding disappointment.

Of course, we all know by now that this was re-enactment. Pure and simple. And it would only be a matter of time before the flashbacks came.

Sure enough, towards the end of August the truth emerged:

> *I was slapped across the face, hard, three times... not in quick succession... But paced. "What have I done wrong?" I pleaded... I knew I was being punished but I didn't know what for.*
>
> *Then I was led towards the box.*
>
> *"No, please... I don't want to go in the box"*
>
> *I was put in the box... It was a really tight one, I was curled right up, my chin was crunched into my chest to fit in the space... It was hard to breathe.*

Yes. That was it. *That's* what I'd been looking for in those cupboards and wardrobes.

> *The lid was closed and I heard the latches snap shut.*

> *I began just breathing as best I could. Just ride it out... It'll be over soon...*
>
> *But it wasn't. Not by any means.*
>
> *I tried to shuffle my body around to get more comfortable but there really wasn't any room to move.*
>
> *I started counting slowly...*

Of course, this flashback was Rachel. You know that by now, right? You recognise the signature.

Sorry... where was I...?

> *I started counting slowly...*
>
> *About one number every two seconds... I lost track a few times as I kinda dissociated further... I didn't know where I was up to... I think I may have skipped numbers... I remember getting up I to the thirties but then I lost count again...*
>
> *I tried pushing against the walls but it wouldn't give. I screamed. Nothing happened. No one came. My leg started cramping. I peed myself.*

I report these things as if they were in quick succession. They weren't. There were long, long uncomfortable minutes between them.

> *I let out angry growls. I tried to surrender to it but the discomfort made that impossible.*
>
> *I tried to sleep. Again, impossible.*

> *After who knows how long—an hour? more?—I heard the latches... the lid was opened, but I didn't trust it so I stayed in position.*
>
> *Someone grabbed my hair and pulled me up out of the box with it.*
>
> *One giant slap across the face and I was pushed back down and the lid closed and locked again.*
>
> *I was crying now. Crying and screaming.*
>
> *What had I done to deserve this?*
>
> *After a while longer I knew I had to get out of the flashback otherwise I'd be trapped in it for ever... I tried a few times to push my way out of the box, but I couldn't, even in real life... but eventually I got an arm free and I could get out of the ordeal.*

Trapped in it for ever. That's the key right there.

For *ever.*

Because that was Amanda's experience.

Rachel—as you can tell from her signature *counting*—was put *in* the box. And Rachel was taken *out* of the box.

But Rachel had limits. As I've mentioned before, she could maybe count up to an hour, but after that, time lost its meaning. It became 'for ever'.

Once Rachel gave up—once she had lost all hope of ever getting rescued—she handed over to Amanda.

And when there was any sign of rescue—footsteps, or latches being opened—she, Rachel, stepped back in, so she could take whatever was to follow.

The box was always used for 'storage' between rounds of abuse. Put in there when not needed. Taken out again when there was more torture to be dealt out.

Rachel took the torture.

But in the box? In that 'for ever'?

The infinite wait?

That was Amanda.

Amanda's experience had no start and no end. Her entire world consisted of six tight wooden walls. Almost completely motionless.

For ever.

It was, strangely, a kind of 'break'. It didn't feel like it to Amanda, necessarily, but when put in context with all the other parts, she wasn't actually being *actively* tortured or violated. There was a *tiny* sense of peace. Or at least *stillness*.

But that didn't invalidate the fact that she—I—was suffering. This *was* a torture, albeit a more passive one.

I asked how long she was in there.

"I don't know."

Hours?

"Maybe."

Was it ever the next day when you came out?

"Yes."

Holy hell.

I started disbelieving this story. And it's with great fear that you do that. You don't want to disbelieve *any* of your girls.

As with all survivors, she has been brave enough to come forward, and her biggest fear is not being believed.

Actually, her biggest fear is being put back there. But a close second is not being believed.

You have to respect that.

But hours? Overnight?

Sometimes you have to believe *her,* even if you can't bring yourself to believe *it.*

It was while I was still deep in this doubt that I learned of Colleen Stan, a survivor who was kidnapped in 1978 and spent *years* locked in a box for twenty-three hours at a time, only being let out for an hour of daily torture.

It's truly awful when you hear other stories of abuse and torture, but when you realise that the outrageous things that happened to you also happened to others it's... comforting? Strange word, I know. But survivors will know what I mean.

You hate that someone else suffered. But you're relieved that it wasn't just you, and more importantly that you're not just completely crazy and fabricating it.

So I believed Amanda.

I did anyway, *really,* but we talked about that beautiful protection mechanism called doubt, right?

I talked about the 'blanked room' in an earlier chapter. I'm pretty sure that was used for the storage — for these boxes.

And I'm pretty sure there was someone else—a boy—who never made it out.

When I first recalled those memories, it was so early in my healing that I thought it *must* be symbolic. There wasn't *really* a boy put in a box, crying and bleeding. There wasn't *really* a limp, lifeless body taken back out of the box an hour or so later. Surely?

But knowing what I know now, of course, I believe it was entirely literal. No symbolism. Just another tragic loss.

❧

Of course, the incident with the boy made Amanda's endless waiting even more traumatic. She wondered if her ordeal would *ever* end. She feared she would die in there.

But to be honest, there wasn't much else for her.

No beginning. No end.

Just countless unmeasured hours confined in the dark.

❧

Then one day when Amanda was showing me the box again, I had a breakthrough. It took a while, but I managed to convince her that she wasn't in the box any more.

Slowly, slowly I convinced her to straighten an arm and discover space. Her arm stretched out fully without touching a boundary.

Incredible.

And the other arm?

Oh my god, the same.

And the legs?

Same again.

Holy crap. This felt *so* weird. She was fronting so strongly. But my *observing self* was right there, encouraging her and directing her.

This world was *alien* to her. A world where the boundaries are wider than your hunched-up limbs? Unthinkable.

But that wasn't all. It became even more tragic. Well — tragic *and* joyful at the same time.

As she explored the space, her hand touched the velour headboard of the bed. She was *fascinated.*

I suddenly realised — *texture.*

She had *never felt texture.*

Her *entire fucking world* existed within the bounds of that box. The only texture she *ever knew* was hard wood.

And now here she was feeling velour. And the smooth curves of the wooden headboard surround.

If you thought the headboard was exciting, you haven't heard the half of it.

The next thing Amanda's hand alighted on? Her fingers reached the paw of my teddy bear.

Holy fucking shit.

It *absolutely blew her away.*

As I've mentioned so many times, doubt is *huge* in trauma recovery. You so often wonder if you're making things up. But then moments like this happen and you know that you *can't* be making it up. A body does *not* respond like this to some fictional musing. It responds like this because it fucking *knows.*

She touched the bear.

She felt the paw.

She had never felt softness like it. It honestly blew her mind.

She started sobbing uncontrollably. You know, the proper 'ugly cry' where you can't breathe, you think you might be sick, but it also feels amazingly cathartic.

She was sobbing with joy at the bear. She pulled it close and held it tight. But she was also sobbing with grief. With the terror and pain of her experience — endured for hours and hours, and then *held silently* for decades.

❧

I knew the box was bad, even *Rachel's* experiences in the boxes were bad. But Amanda's were truly on another level.

Even outside the box, she tries to take up as little space as possible. I think that echoed into my daily life.

But even with her horrific ordeals, I am so pleased that she was able to experience joy. And what *incredible* joy that was.

Honestly, to this day, Amanda still reaches out and touches things if the texture looks inviting. And I let her. And I experience her joy *with* her.

I feel privileged to have been present with her as she reached out and touched that teddy bear for the first time.

Truly privileged.

# 16. Stinky-Poo

Speaking of teddy bears... that brings me to Stinky-Poo.

I was talking with my therapist one day, I can't remember how we got on the subject, but I talked about my childhood teddy bear. And it was *as I was describing him* that the horror dawned on me.

I was realising what incredibly shitty parents I had. In real-time. As the words came out of my mouth.

My bear, my main comfort object as a child, wasn't a nice plump, soft animal. He was a hand-me-down from my much-older cousin who used to wet the bed, and this poor bear had received his fair share of soaking.

His stuffing was rotten and hard, his fur was matted and bare in places. I clearly remember the indignant expression he had on his face... the kind *you* would have if you'd spent as many nights as he did getting soaked in urine.

And so his most prominent feature—the feature I named him after—was indeed, the fact that he *absolutely stank. Of piss.*

Of course he did.

Stale, years-old piss, right through to his core.

We washed him. We doused him in perfume. But that distinctive stench of piss always prevailed. That's why I named him 'Stinky-Poo'.

I was quite fond of him. I guess that's what you'd expect if he was your only source of comfort.

But let's just rewind a moment.

My parents.

My parents were thinking about a bear to give to their daughter. Their darling daughter.

And they made a conscious decision and said "Yes. Cousin Neil's stinking piss-soaked sorry-ass bear will do. That's all she's fucking worth."

They might not have used those exact words, but that's the message they sent, loud and clear, into my three-year-old psyche.

Here... have piss-soaked scraps.

Of course, Stinky-Poo wasn't the *only* indication I had of my lack of worth... there were many, many more, but this one really stands out to me. One of those things a child *should* have... a comfort object. Something to cuddle when times are tough, when you can't sleep, when you've dropped your ice-cream or when been told off for drawing on the wallpaper again (no, I didn't draw on the wallpaper — my god, can you imagine?)

I was only recently in a shop with my best friend and we passed a gorgeous plushie.

I stopped. I began to caress his fur, rub his ear between my fingers. Soothe the back of his paw.

My friend gave me the compassionate look of someone launching a gentle intervention, and said, "You don't need any more plushies".

My retort?

"Girl, I had a piss-soaked thread-bare teddy as my *only comfort* in my childhood, I get to buy whatever the fuck plushies I want now!"

She nodded respectfully.

"Of *course* you do. Fair point."

# 17. Debbie

Peace at last!

In the last twenty-one days, eleven parts had shown up — three weeks of chaotic hell. I'd relived Rebecca and Kat's tortures, Amanda's time in the box, Eve and Melissa's programming—more on that soon—and many more fragments based around Laura's trafficking.

But here I was, kneeling on a blanket, completely at peace with myself.

Well… not myself. I was in Melanie's flashback.

I say peace — I mean, I was naked. I was alone in a concrete cell I didn't recognise. And there was a steel collar around my neck, chained to a ring in the floor.

But I was at peace.

❧

It was a strange flashback. Several flashbacks in a row, actually, spread over several days.

Each one was very similar. I could feel the steel collar around my neck, even in the present moment. And I could feel that beautiful peace.

But what I *couldn't* feel was any *context.*

Most of my flashbacks came with context built-in. I'd know instantly... this is a hotel room, this is my father, this is a 'Rachel' thing...

But with Melanie? Nothing.

Sometimes I was kneeling. Sometimes I was lying on the thin blanket — the only thing protecting me from the cold, bare concrete floor.

But always at peace.

I slowly realised what the peace was about...

It was the lack of performance. The lack of expectations.

A little like Amanda's experience—although hers was horribly restricted—Melanie's experience was a break from the norm.

While I was there, alone, I wasn't being tortured. And I wasn't being violated. I wasn't having to fawn to strange men. And I wasn't having to guess when the next blow of a cane, or the next shock was coming from.

I could just sit or lie there, breathe, and... dare I say it? *Relax.*

That relaxation? It was very real. And I sought it so many times in my later life.

I can't remember the first time I bought a steel collar in adulthood, I think it was my early twenties. But the moment I locked it in place, I just felt *safe*. Held. Peaceful.

That cold steel. Unforgiving.

Of course, I didn't know *why* I'd bought it. It just seemed like a good idea. It seemed to draw me by some invisible force.

And I didn't know why it felt so peaceful either. But it did.

I even attached a ring to the floor and bought a length of chain to lock myself to. Pretty dangerous, actually. I mean, I never let the key get out of reach, but if I had, I may not have been here to write this book.

That's what I craved, really. The *inescapable.* I didn't know, at the time, that this was a mirror of my childhood, but it was such a powerful craving.

I thought about posting myself a key, then locking myself within reach of the letterbox. Having to wait quietly a few days for release.

Of course, if the key got lost in the post? That's one dead Georgia, and that's why I never did it. As always, safety first.

And as I've alluded to in other chapters about the re-enactments, that was one of the biggest disappointments: I played safely, but the *accuracy* I was looking for wasn't safe at all.

I had consent (even if it was misguided and programmed) and I had a get-out. My child self had none of that.

I talked about the cycle of accumulation and shameful purging of kit in the chapter on fetishes. The steel collar? One of the main culprits. I don't want to think how many hundreds, maybe *thousands* of pounds I spent on steel shackles.

But I kept buying them because some part of me thought that the stillness meant love. Or peace. Or something altogether different, but still important.

So in my flashbacks—in Melanie's memory, and somatic response—I had found this peace. But of course, the situation, especially the *location,* still bothered me...

I first called it a 'cellar', but later figured out that 'cell' was a better description. I didn't know if it was underground or not. I just know it was a bare, concrete room. Not small, but not large... the size doesn't really feature in my flashbacks but I didn't feel confined in there. Or lost.

But one question bugged me:

*Who owned the cell?*

Throughout my discovery process, I kept a running list of unanswered questions. I'd write down things that were bugging me, little clues I'd picked up... anything that seemed too significant to ignore, but not significant enough to obsess over — the sort of question I knew would be answered by parts when they were ready:

> *Who was at the flat in London when I was fourteen?*
>
> *Who underwent electrical torture?*
>
> *Why are [insert name of abuser]'s freezers so important?*

*Who owned the cell?*

There it was.

The list was longer than this, of course. Some of the items are now answered to my satisfaction — the first one will come up later and you already know about Kat and the electrical torture. The freezers? Still unanswered.

But that cell?

*Who owned the cell?*

And why was I left there?

I don't know how long I was in there, exactly. It feels like a long weekend, maybe? It could be less, it could be much more. With no clocks, no daylight and no changes to the room lighting it's hard to tell.

I don't know exactly how long I was left *alone,* either. But it was a long time. Likely measured in hours. Many hours.

Why? What was the purpose?

I'd often had flashbacks to Laura's time between clients — lying there bound to the bed by my wrists, nothing happening. Bored. Wondering why she was even bothering to show me this!

But at least Laura's long waits had purpose — the next client was on his way.

This one? I didn't know.

What was the point of my being chained to the floor and left on a blanket for hours?

I don't think I have ever answered that question.

I was left for hours. Alone.

For whose benefit?

Who was *enjoying* this?

And why?

I never figured out *why*, but I did figure out *who.*

It hit me one day. I think I was just going about my business, maybe watching dumb kitten videos on YouTube, I honestly can't remember.

Oh shit.

It hit me...

Fuck!

This is Debbie...

Shit.

Debbie had emerged some eight days *before* Melanie.

She is another one of my parts who gave me the most horrendously terrifying flashbacks. And it was strange because nothing 'bad' really happened to her.

While Julia's flashbacks had embodied the sheer *pain and violation* of Laura's experiences in the hotel rooms, Debbie's distress was based on a *promise.*

And it's times like this, as I'm writing the book, that I am *so* fucking pleased that I logged every one of my flashbacks.

I logged them as soon as I could after I came back to the room — back to the present moment in my own body.

It works because when I don't want to revisit what happened —when I don't want to live through it all again—I can simply pull the flashback report from my archive and paste it wherever I need to. This manuscript, for example.

I don't mind reading it again, but to *write* it again? I'm not ready for that.

Here's what I journaled on that day in September when Debbie emerged. As with so many emergence experiences, it started with doubt—and with fragmented memory—before Debbie had actually felt safe enough to make herself known:

> *The caged girl still hasn't shown herself. I'm beginning to doubt the memory I had... a large cage made out of box-section steel, square bars (like squared paper pattern, not just vertical)... checker-plate base with simple blankets... the clang of the hatch as it's opened and closed, and the clang when poles are stuck through the bars to prod my fellow victims into the right place... the misery in there... the other victims... each of us written on... with a lot number?... an auction?*

> *I don't know... a cage to 'pick your lobster' from? I don't know what was happening in that place but I feel it and I see it... and I can't believe it's real but why would I make up a cage design that I've never seen before, especially when I assumed that my caging experiences were on my own...?*
>
> *I think the audience gets to me. I've watched porn where there's an audience... well-dressed people, wealthy, in their best evening wear, watching as a woman is abused... I can't watch those videos... it's the audience that does it... one-on-one I can watch (though it's getting harder and harder to not recognise the suffering - I'm starting to lose the numbness and be unable to watch any kind of porn)...*
>
> *But ones with an audience... privileged people gawking over abuse... it's fucking horrible.*
>
> *It's probably mirroring something that really happened to me.*

This is *exactly* how trauma memory works... the fragments, the partly-known truths, the triggers in later life... you can clearly see here how it's a *forensic* task of joining the fragments into an understandable whole.

And it's all infused with that fucking *doubt* that relentlessly permeates the experience.

❧

And can we just acknowledge the *audience* for a moment? These truly seem to be a couple of the things I struggle with most, even now: the photos and the audiences.

I think it's because it's not just the suffering. Not just the torture. Not just the violation and pain.

It's the fact you become a *spectacle,* you become a *souvenir.*

It's one thing to suffer in your own private world, but to have that suffering *shared* for entertainment? Honestly, that's a whole new level, and one that I—and many other survivors I've spoken to—struggle with greatly.

My father was always very intrusive with a video camera even in conscious memory — this was after the divorce when I had blanked him less. I can't imagine what he was like with it in private.

❧

Anyway, back to Debbie.

About thirty minutes after the first revelations I'd had, things started to become much clearer:

> *Oh my god.*
>
> *She's called Debbie.*
>
> *I'm there in the cage. Large, filled with other victims. I don't know... ten others? All naked, all with numbers written on their bodies.*
>
> *It feels so horrible... in real life I'm screaming into my pillow... the screams I wasn't allowed to let*

*out then... the vulnerability... the cold steel... the fucking AUDIENCE... lots of well-dressed people, men and women, in their evening-wear... looking privileged, aloof and condescending...*

*I don't know what's worse, the shame of being naked, the discomfort of being cold, the despair that I have no escape, the vulnerability of all the eyes on me, or the sheer despair at being commodified... not a person, a* product.

*But if I thought I was screaming before? I discovered something way worse...*

*I was chosen... I was picked... the cage was opened and I was lifted out...*

*Holy fucking shit... my screaming went to an intensity I've never experienced. I've never experienced terror like that before, even with all of my trauma memory so far... knowing that I'm being handed to cruel people (a man and woman) who I already know will do the most unthinkable things to me...*

*I can hardly even fucking WRITE it... I honestly don't know what they did... I'll have to rely on another part to report that... but the abject TERROR of being picked out of the cage... a hundred times worse than actually being in there.*

*There's no "let's please them" of Laura here... it is defenceless, powerless, I know that my immediate future contains searing pain and degradation and there is nothing I can fucking do about it.*

*Luckily my observing self could step in (I actually did several times throughout)... "It's okay, Debbie... let it out... you're safe now... it's okay to let it out..." And she did.*

*Honestly, those early screams when I first recovered my memories? The way they shook my soul and made me realise this wasn't just imagination or fantasy... this had the same effect... even after all this time, when I shouldn't be able to be surprised by what comes up, I was fucking surprised at those screams...*

*It's about twenty minutes later now, and I'm still shaking.*

❧

If you need to take a break right now, please do. I'm going to make a cup of tea and have a mint Cornetto.

❧

I'm back.

I talked a little bit about what healing looks like in the introduction to the book, but since I've just done a full self-care-when-triggered routine, let's talk about it in detail. This is the real deal, reported straight after the fact...

So... the break. You might not even know you're triggered, but you know something is feeling off.

You go to your kitchen, put the kettle on and get an ice-cream out of the freezer. You eat the ice-cream while making the tea one-handed. This gives you the time separation between cold and hot to avoid that searing dental pain of thermal shock (also known in medical fields as '*instant regret*')

You accidentally pull a broken teabag out of the jar and don't notice until you've poured tea-leaves all over the counter-top. You make a half-hearted effort to clean it up, while the back of your mind mutters "Later, babe. Later."

You take the milk out of the fridge and notice the half of a jacket potato you put in there several days ago, fully intending to eat it at some point, but never quite finding the right time. You know it will go in the bin[13], but don't actually put it in the bin. That would be admitting defeat.

You go back to your office, ice-cream finished and tea in hand and you fire up YouTube. You check your '*smile*' folder and decide on "Orpheus in the Underworld" by the Teddy Bears Marimba Trio[14]. Cute. You smile. Good job — the folder name checks out!

Then you lock your screen and sip your tea in silence with your eyes closed. You're hugging the cup for warmth and safety, and whispering phrases such as "oh gosh" and "fucking hell" as Debbie's reality lands and you slowly realise—as

13 Three hours later, I scooped the potato out of the skin, mixed it with butter and grated cheese, refilled the skin and grilled it until it was a delicious, crispy, greasy, cheesy mess. Next book, coming soon: *Georgia's Easy Recipes for Barely-Functioning Survivors.*

14 Honestly. I am not making this up — https://youtu.be/miFCWJDjL1w

you have time and time again—that it was literally *you* there, not 'Debbie'.

You regulate your breathing as best you can to avoid getting pulled back into that room, that horrible cage. Deep belly breaths that you learnt in your mindfulness classes all those years ago.

You continue with the expletives. This is important. "Jesus *Christ*". The more creative the better. *"Fucking shitbags"*...

It's only ten in the morning, but you go to your bedroom where the curtains are still closed and the covers, pillows and plushies are strewn around because of this morning's flash-back — the one where you literally had to crawl out of the foot-end of the bed to force it to end.

You jump in your bed and grab your big, body-sized plushie. And you *hold* that plushie. Tight.

You sob quietly and repeat as often as necessary:

"Debbie I love you... you're safe now"

Over and over. Until she gets the message and you feel your nervous system start to relax just a little.

You decide that today isn't going to be the day you get your groceries after all. You have bread and instant ramen and eggs in the cupboard. Maybe a few other essentials. You'll survive. You always have so far. Maybe you'll go at eleven o'clock tonight—as you so often do — when the supermarket is a quiet other-world of produce-cages, shelf-stackers and other lost and healing souls.

Then after an hour in the warm safety of your bed—maybe scrolling, maybe doing puzzles, maybe just lying there in the darkness, maybe having a nap or two—you notice yourself slowly, slowly coming back online.

You notice normal feeling coming back, like you're starting to inhabit your body again, instead of being wherever you had dissociated to.

You notice that your need for a pee is suddenly more important than your desire to remain inert. You wish you were wearing a diaper so you could just *go.*

You aren't, so you take a few deep breaths, give a deep sigh and say one last, heartfelt "fucking hell!"

You give your plushie the biggest squeeze and re-iterate: "Debbie, I love you. You are safe now."

And finally you get up, go for that pee, drink some water, and you go about your day...

Well... you kinda go about your day.

It's about an hour later that you wake up properly and notice that you're here, and alive, and can feel, and the world *actually* seems fully real again.

That is what healing looks like. It takes time. It has to be gentle. You have suffered enough violence in your lifetime. Now it's time for peace. Self-love. Self-care. Always.

Of course, as I've mentioned before, no-one hands you a manual on how to do this stuff, so I daresay other survivors have *completely* different ways of handling this uncomfortable, ungrounded, dissociated state.

But that's how I do it. And it works.

Softness isn't weakness. Slowness isn't laziness.

Self-care isn't self-indulgence.

It's vital. Life-saving.

And I no longer apologise for it.

❧

So Debbie was picked. She immediately handed over to Fiona for what happened next. I won't go into a great amount of detail, but she was forced to perform for the rest of the evening — both with the couple who 'won' her, and with the other victims. And all for the benefit of the assembled audience.

And when the evening was over? That's where the memory goes blank again, until it wakes up in Melanie's shoes. Well, you know what I mean — if she was *wearing* shoes.

The couple in question—and this is the first and only time I experienced a female perpetrator—didn't just win me for the night. They didn't just get my domestic and sexual service for that evening. No. They took me home. To their private cell.

That was the "Oh Fuck" moment I had while trying to figure out Melanie.

That's why I was struggling to place the cell in my mind. It's why it didn't connect with any of the other experiences.

The cell belonged to fucking *strangers* — strangers who had won me in some sort of auction, and now had the privilege of taking me home to do whatever they wanted with me. A new type of private hell.

❧

It took the longest time to get past Melanie, though. I knew for *so long* that she didn't hold the whole experience. There was *no way* I was taken to a private cell just to be abandoned there for however long. (I talk about a weekend, but that, honestly, is a complete guess. It could have been a week. It could have been more. Trauma and dissociation don't really treat time in the same way most people are accustomed to.)

I realised I'd been acting pretty strangely for a week or two. I'd been getting obsessed with bodily functions. Feeling weird about it. Berating myself. Feeling shame.

And then the penny dropped.

I let go of the shame. I told myself it's okay. I realised that these behaviours may *well* be re-enactments of abuse.

And sure enough, with that acceptance and self-love, Holly was finally happy to show herself.

I won't detail what happened to me in that cell that I passed on to Holly to bear, but it was truly different from anything else that had happened before now.

I was chained the whole time. Out of the couple who had won me, I only ever saw the woman once we moved from the 'event' to the cell.

And oh *my*, did she have some interesting and creative obsessions about bodily functions. And was she ever willing to share those obsessions with me.

Ugh.

❧

It took me a while to realise that the cage was real. It took a while to come to terms with the fact that abuse doesn't just happen in dingy rooms with sleazy abusers.

No, it can also happen in grand, organised events with well-dressed people making a spectacle of the whole thing. With those who fancy themselves as 'civilised society', inflicting the most unthinkable humiliation and horror on defenceless children. Of *course* that happens. We'd just rather ignore it.

Those events are real. Too real.

But you know what else is real?

Tea. Duvets. Plushies.

I am no longer in those rooms. I am here, now.

And while their echoes still vibrate in my bones and my nervous system, I am slowly learning that there is life *after* the abuse.

This is integration. This is the journey. This is healing.

# 18. Economics

I never saw any of the money change hands.

Of course I didn't.

This wasn't sleazy individuals in dingy hotel rooms making a side-hustle. It was *organised.*

There were leaders, there were those who were experts in breaking children's minds and programming them, there were enforcers, and there were handlers—wranglers—men who were there to make sure the victims were in the right place, stayed where they were meant to be, and were prepared for the ordeals.

I remember one flashback which didn't make sense at all. It was in a hotel. But I wasn't tied. And it wasn't a client.

I realised after a while that this was a casual, opportunist rape from one of my handlers. Incredible. The boss is out of the room for ten minutes... time for my fun.

Asshole.

Anyway... back to the subject, Georgia...

With all these roles, I have to assume there were cashiers and treasurers. The money didn't change hands in the hotel rooms, it probably went under the table in a brown envelope, days or weeks before in a bar, or over a dinner somewhere.

No, I didn't see the money at all.

But I saw the *results* of the money. That was unmissable.

The houses. The cars. The wealth that didn't fit.

It really struck me one day recently when I realised that one of my friends' parents had largely the same jobs as my own parents. But their living situations were so different.

Don't get me wrong, my friend's parents were comfortable. Really nicely comfortable. Being of the boomer generation, they owned their home, mortgage paid off, good pensions, a couple of holidays a year, no *real* worries about heating or groceries or home repairs.

But they were living in the three bed semi-detached house that they had bought over thirty years ago.

I mean, that is *so* normal, right? It's what you expect. The middle-class ideal. Comfortable life. Nice house. Warm, dry, room for family to come round.

My father?

The house we lived in when I was born fitted the bill perfectly. Suburban semi-detached. Similar people round the neighbourhood.

The next house we bought? When I was three? When I had already met the network and been subjected to a not insignificant amount of suffering?

Well, it was a large, detached four bed property. The largest on the street. Ostentatious. Enough so that people knew you as the family that lived in the big house.

Over time, his houses and cars only grew in prestige and value. Not too long ago I was blown away by hearing he spent four hundred pounds to fix an indicator bulb.

He flexed on his wealth too. Probably still does, it's just that I'm not in contact now.

Sure, he worked hard. He did some work that paid premium prices. But it still didn't add up.

And his friends. Other people that I've identified within the network. Again, houses and living situations that just *don't add up* given their jobs.

And this wasn't generational wealth. It was rapid growth — new money.

And always a large, detached house. The sort you can disappear into without questions being asked. The sort with rooms that no-one ever goes in.

There could have been innocent explanations. I will likely never know. But I'm just saying, along with all the other evidence, this didn't add up.

The clues are everywhere, sometimes overt, sometimes less obvious. You can easily dismiss one or two of them, but those dots that I seem to *love* mentioning? Well, they begin to join, and when they do, you can't un-join them.

One such dot was my father's seeming obsession for always pointing out places that were likely to be laundering money. I have the habit myself, now, of spotting them and calling them out.

Like, why would that even be a thing? Why would you a) *have* that knowledge, and b) *need* that knowledge?

Unless...

Yeah. Unless you were using them?

I don't know.

❧

It was actually money that led me on this *whole* quest.

Accidentally. Indirectly.

I'd been seeing my therapist for about fourteen months and had *really* done well letting go of my Complex PTSD from the emotional abuse I had suffered from my mother.

Interestingly, my therapist always said I had *declared* that I had CPTSD, but I never *presented* to her as if I had CPTSD. Thank you, Emily... good job — your mask was impeccable! Once the abuse emerged and I allowed Emily to drop her façade, she said I presented *exactly* as someone with CPTSD!

Anyway...

I'd rebuilt my identity. Discovered boundaries — and started setting and honouring them like a queen. I'd learnt that it was okay to express myself, that I wasn't *shameful* simply for being me. I'd learnt to know what I wanted and what I definitely *didn't* want.

Honestly, I was doing *really* well.

I even stopped my sessions, gave my therapist a thank-you card, and we parted company on wonderful terms with an open invitation to come back any time.

It was only a month or so later I realised something...

Yes, I was so happy with who I was. I'd discovered self-love. I had direction in life. I was functioning well.

I still wasn't *earning any money.*

When I'd burnt out some two and a half years earlier, I took a sabbatical. No pressure to earn. Just live on savings and heal whatever needed healing.

Now I was 'fixed'. But I still wasn't earning.

Something was still amiss, clearly.

So I contacted my therapist and asked if she thought we might be able to have a quick course of six sessions just to sort out a single issue: my money mindset.

Holy fuck, right?

If only I knew then what I know now...

Poor, naïve girl!

We started working together and while money mindset *was* clearly an issue, the little background niggle about my grandfather came up. Did he abuse me? You know, was there a slim chance that on, like, *one occasion,* he might have had access and done something?

You already know that part of the story.

But what I didn't realise was that this *was* solving the money mindset problem. It was all wrapped up in the same trauma.

I'd done all the courses. Read all the books. I knew how money mindset worked... you had to stop seeing money as evil and see it as love.

You had to love it into your life.

Nothing I was being taught resonated. I couldn't put my finger on it, but no matter how many times I talked to myself in the mirror, or listened to night-time affirmations, nothing changed. Nothing.

It was only through the process of uncovering Laura and Debbie that I realised...

I was never taught that money was evil. That's poverty thinking. That's what *most* people with money issues suffer from (if the gurus are to be believed — I'm sceptical about *everything* the gurus tell us).

But I didn't have that issue. I *knew* money was good. I knew all the nice things you could buy with money. I'd *seen* them.

I knew it bought you freedom. I knew it bought you comfort and safety. I knew it bought you *choice.*

What a *wonderful* thing!

No, the problem wasn't that money was evil.

Money was absolutely *wonderful.* The problem was that *I didn't deserve a single penny of it because I was a worthless piece of shit.*

They'd told me so.

That was the real issue. And it went deep, and would require more therapy and more time to work on.

❧

All through my adult life, long before I knew anything about my abuse, I thought about doing sex work. I knew I'd be good at it—excellent, in fact—but I also knew I would die inside. And maybe in body too.

With what I know now, it's kind of obvious, isn't it?

I also know now what an *incredible* betrayal of my girls it would be: putting them back through the violation they already survived once.

For most of my life, though, it felt like the only option I had to earn and thrive. That's not uncommon for survivors.

The lie was strong: *My only value is in being violated. And the more degrading the violation, the higher the worth.*

Wow. Go me, right? That's true empowerment — but only if you're traumatised to hell and back.

I am *so fucking glad* I never took that route — not because it's shameful or wrong, but because for me it would have been a death sentence. Whether that sentence came from a violent client, or from the slow self-abandonment that would have followed.

Either way, it would have killed me.

❧

My father was financially controlling all my life, and I had somewhat built a dependency on him. It was designed that way, I'm quite sure.

I tried to earn my own way through life. And I *almost* made it. *Almost* all of the time. But it never quite clicked.

I felt *guilty,* honestly, for earning money when I was a computer programmer. My company was selling million-pound-plus systems, and I was feeling *guilty* about my £30k.

I was made redundant from that job in 2008 and went self-employed.

And once I was self-employed, I gave so much of myself away for free it's not funny.

They say *don't give away the farm.* Dammit, I gave away not only the farm, but the mineral rights, the lifetime royalties and my fucking soul.

I ended up—for a few years before my sabbatical—working for deluded, narcissistic CEOs so I could *still* express a comfortable level of fawning to powerful men, while receiving all the emotional abuse I thought I deserved.

I ran their companies as a chief operating officer, easily a six-figure job — and I accepted £30k for the privilege. It truly appears that £30k is—or hopefully *was*—my absolute emotional ceiling!

I didn't *fail to attract money,* I fucking *rejected it* at every opportunity. I bled myself dry, took the abuse, and didn't even get any kind of reward. Just like in the hotel rooms, you dumb bitch.

Now hold up, there, Georgia! Remember. No blame. No shame. This wasn't your fault... you were doing the best you could with a traumatised brain and nervous system. I love you. You are safe now. And you are not a dumb bitch.

Thank you. Thank you for catching that. You always have to catch it when self-hate rears its head. Catch it and counter it with love and acceptance. Well done, I'm proud of you!

Now, where was I? Ah yes, rejecting money...

And because I was rejecting money, it kept me dependent on hand-outs from my father. Convenient, that.

But they were always on *his* terms. Random timing. Random amounts. Never promised.

In psychological circles, this is known as *intermittent reinforcement* and it's put to powerful use in slot machines, social media and abusive relationships. It's proven to build a strong dependency in those who are vulnerable.

You're caught in an endless loop of 'maybe *this* time...'

This dependency I had developed—correction: *that was instilled in me*—was one of the most significant sources of shame I dealt with.

What kind of adult woman depends on financial hand-outs from her fucking father?

I'll tell you: a *traumatised* one who has been indoctrinated with *learned helplessness.*

*That* kind of adult woman.

Specifically, *this* adult woman.

But it still felt so shameful. And a while after the abuse emerged I contacted him for reparations.

He pleaded ignorance, but did pay up (I had asked for a degradingly low sum, and he agreed to half of that)

I felt *so much* like I was scrounging. Like I was asking for money that I had no right to — shamefully begging for something I absolutely didn't deserve.

I spoke about it with my survivors' group, and that's when my mindset began to change.

I had been talking about the shame, and also the *privilege* of financial dependence. *Double* shame. Not only that I, a grown-ass woman, was dependent on my fucking father for money, but also the guilt that *many* survivors don't even get close to that opportunity.

I knew that I *should* be earning my keep. I *should* be supporting myself.

My group put me straight — *good* group!

> *"Firstly, you're* not *a grown-ass woman. You're a survivor. 'Should' doesn't apply when you're a survivor. The fact that you are here, and breathing, is a fucking miracle."*

This is the kind of straight-talk I appreciate.

> *"Secondly... it's* your *fucking money that you're asking for."*

This one floored me. But they were right.

> *"You did really well at your job in those hotel rooms, even if it wasn't a job you wanted. And they* stole *your income from you."*

Shit.

Yes. They did.

And Debbie's experience?

I don't know the exact sums involved, but you do *not* get to 'win' a trained, stretched, programmed and compliant child in an auction and take them home to your private dungeon for however long I was there, without a *very large sum of money* changing hands. A *very large sum indeed.*

I never saw a fucking penny of that. Nor any of the money from the hotels.

My best guess is that it's easily seven figures, distributed between leaders, handlers, trainers and... my father. You know, the father with the big house and fancy car?

The father with the big house and fancy car while I'm struggling to make ends meet due to the trauma that has plagued my whole fucking fifty years on the planet?

Him.

My survivors' group continued their loving onslaught...

> *"You worked hard, you paid with your body, your soul, your dignity, and they diverted* your *income into* their own *pockets. You were already financially independent. Your independence was intercepted by blood-sucking leeches."*

Fuck. They were *still* right.

Damn.

And it wasn't just the money, directly. The connections. The opportunities. The status. All gained from my suffering and violation, my tears, my screams.

It's a harsh reality to bear, and it's still going to take work to overcome. But this mindset shift has been so vital.

I am not a *victim.* I am a *survivor.* Very different. A victim stays stuck. A survivor moves forward. Despite the pain. *Because* of the pain. Whatever. A survivor moves forward.

I realised the truth: not one *single* penny my father has given me has *anything* to do with generosity. It has *everything* to do with silence, forced dependency and control.

And it hasn't got *close* to the sums I now have receipts for.

Not paper receipts, obviously.

But I know.

And he knows.

*Sarah carries the memory of witnessing murder.*
*This chapter contains graphic emotional content.*

# 19. Sarah

*He was behind me. He was holding me firmly upright with one arm, and pressing the point of a large, sharp knife into my abdomen.*

*I was shaking with fear...*

*"No shaking"*

*"Yes, sir". I did my best to breathe steadily and hold still even though I was terrified.*

*"Relax your shoulders"*

*"Yes, sir"... I didn't relax them—I couldn't—but I did consciously lower them.*

*The pressure on the knife increased a little. I had no doubt that he would push it in if I did anything wrong.*

*"So you're going to do exactly as you're told?"*

*"Yes, sir"*

If you're reading this in a marathon session, it might be wise to take another break here. Sarah's story is heavy. And sharp. If you've just made it through Debbie and the economics, your body might need a breath. That's okay. I'll still be here when you come back.

❧

Now where were we?

*"So you're going to do exactly as you're told?"*

*"Yes, sir"*

I couldn't remember the words after this... there were just a few more threats or instructions and more "Yes, sir". I felt like my voice was quivering but I couldn't afford to let that show. I had to be in total control of myself despite the terror.

My observing self recognised what was happening.

"Melissa?" — she didn't reply but I knew it was her.

The flashback continued beyond this point, but there was something wrong — it was totally blank. I was still *there* but had no sight or sound, no feelings, nothing. I was dissociated into a void.

I knew this must be serious.

I asked Melissa, "Do you want to show me?"

She said "I've already shown you too much"

I conceded: "Yes. You've shown me enough, Melissa. I understand. You're safe now. Those men can't find you."

And the flashback released me.

❧

Melissa was charged with running the programs and scripts they installed. I guessed that this incident was showing me how those programs and scripts were reinforced. Melissa was certainly *terrified* of the men and the knives.

Melissa was the fourteenth part to emerge. But there was something very *different* about her emergence.

Every other part so far carried some awful trauma — more than any one person could cope with, hence why they split off in the first place.

I was compassionate and loving towards them. I cared for them. I listened to their reports, and witnessed what they wanted me to see. I assured them they were safe and loved. I couldn't see any other way to treat them.

That was until Melissa.

I was lying in the bath, just idly popping bubbles when she emerged. I had been talking with other survivors of ritual abuse—people who were further along in their healing journey—and I was pondering my recent sleep deprivation.

For weeks, no *months,* I had been waking up at the most ungodly hours. Not just waking up, but it felt like I was being *woken up* — by an outside agent.

One of the survivors made a suggestion... is it possible that your sleep deprivation is programmed into you? They knew. They had also experienced programming at the hands of a ritual abuse network.

So that's what I was pondering in the bath... not to any great depth... not expecting an instant answer...

Suddenly, the name 'Melissa' came to me. Just like that. Out of the blue.

I tentatively asked "Melissa? Is that you running the programs?"

She hesitated… then nodded. I could feel how reluctant she was to admit her existence — like even being acknowledged was dangerous for her. So I didn't press.

I already knew about some of the systems she managed. The kill-switch. The sleep deprivation. The urination cue — a specific, conditioned response that bypasses my control. I won't say how it's triggered, just that it leaves me with no choice. If activated, it happens, no matter where I am or what I want.

There was also the honesty trigger — a phrase that makes it physically impossible for me to lie. And again, no, I won't reveal the words.

But I couldn't help wondering what else she held. What other programs were running without my knowledge. I knew she'd tell me, if and when she felt safe enough.

But the main problem?

I found it so hard to *love* Melissa.

I knew I had to but I couldn't.

I talked with my survivors' group:

> *Here's the problem: because she is affecting my life* right now, *I find it hard to have compassion and meet her with love.*
>
> *I hate her.*
>
> *And I know that won't help my healing. It certainly won't help her to trust me enough to realise she can let go of the programs.*
>
> *And because I hate her, I hate myself for being unable to accept her.*
>
> *I know I'll come round but when you're surviving on three, maybe four hours of sleep a night, it's hard to make sensible, rational or compassionate decisions.*
>
> *I'm just sick of this shit. I don't know how to make it stop other than "keep breathing, keep going..." you know "the way out is through" kinda thing.*

That's the problem with healing. You can know *exactly* how you should be handling it, but can still be unable to *actually* do it.

I hated her for such a long time.

But eventually I recognised her as the victim she is.

She didn't want to be running the programs any more than I wanted to be obeying them.

She was *terrified.*

I think I was trying to reconcile my issues with knives when I left the coloured pencils and sketch pad out on the kitchen table. It wasn't long before Melissa had drawn a picture. It showed her waking me up noisily, while two men in suits threatened her with knives.

Yes. She was terrified alright.

The incident with the knife that I opened the chapter with? That was how she was programmed. It got darker. *Way* darker. I will talk briefly about that later.

But for sure, she was a victim. Obligated to run the programs for fear of literal death.

What did happen, though, was that I began to show Melissa that I *saw* her, and that I did, in fact, love her.

When she felt that, she softened.

She never stopped running the programs—way too risky—but she did start to give me a little gentle nudge whenever she began running one.

It was so surreal. And still is.

I would start doing some uncharacteristic or uncalled for behaviour, and a quiet voice would say *"psst... Georgia. It's a program."*

Thank you Melissa.

As I prepare the final edits of the book, I am once again reminded of how *persistent* the programming is. It was a quiet Friday afternoon and I was musing on my boundaries and values, on how I don't owe access to anyone who doesn't provide value and *mutuality* to any particular relationship or interaction. I came to some empowering conclusions and felt more confident in my ability to take my new life forward.

And what should happen? Just ten minutes later, I am in a full activation of the programming. "She's developing boundaries — destroy her", says the program. And I am recreating the punishment and degradation that I was subjected to forty years ago.

Of course, this has happened throughout my life — filled with distress and shame. It has caused me to shrink back. If boundaries come at *this* cost, it's not worth having them. Just continue abandoning yourself and you can avoid the pain and suffering.

The difference now? And this is a testament to healing...

Healing isn't about being *done* with the programs and the triggers and the behaviours. It's absolutely in how you *handle* them. And now, rather than being filled with shame, I simply observe. I'm fascinated.

“Incredible”, I say to myself... “Incredible how programs installed forty years ago can still activate as if they were fresh from yesterday.”

I refuse to feel shame. I refuse to feel distress. I recognise it not as regression, but as activation. Maybe Melissa has given me that little nudge.

So I let it pass through me. I process it. And slowly it loses its power.

Maybe one day the programs will stop running entirely. Maybe they won’t. But one thing is for sure, they don’t hijack my attempts to live my life any more. They don’t cause me to shrink. They don’t hurt me any more.

That’s why they created Melissa in me — to hurt me. And, ultimately, they failed.

❧

Eve was another matter. Another programmed part. But rather than being programmed to harm *me,* she was programmed to harm *others.*

Don’t worry — she doesn’t activate automatically, and the harm is *very* specific and needs props that I don’t have. You are *entirely* safe if we are in the same room.

Basically, more than one of Rachel’s reports talk about the cutting — being cut with a scalpel on the abdomen or thighs. Not deep enough to open a full wound, but deep enough to bleed. And deep enough to suffer excruciating pain when the liquid is rubbed in the cuts.

I have never figured out what the liquid was, but other survivors of ritual abuse report very similar experiences.

Eve? She was trained to do the cutting.

> *I'm in the ritual room (I don't know what that means but it feels like the right word)... There is a girl laid out, strapped to the black board.*
>
> *They give me a blade and a small bottle of pungent liquid.*
>
> *They are right behind me. I am under no illusions that I have to do what they trained me to do.*
>
> *I look into her eyes... I have to... that's part of the orders...*
>
> *I feel like mine are dead, hers are filled with panic. She is so innocent. We are about the same age... Maybe eight? It's hard to tell.*
>
> *Then I pull her dress up to expose her thighs.*
>
> *I make long, deliberate vertical cuts in her thighs. Not too deep. But significant enough to draw blood. I have to hold her leg still because she is writhing.*
>
> *She is sobbing quietly but I think she has been told to stay still and keep quiet.*

> *I feel mechanical. Like I get no joy nor horror from what I'm doing. I just have a job to do. Refusing doesn't occur to me.*
>
> *After each cut, I put a little of the liquid on my fingers and I rub it over the wound. I've had this done to me and I know how much it stings. She screams each time.*
>
> *The flashback only lasts for a few cuts before it becomes too much and I come out of it.*

Even though I know Eve was forced to do this, it was still so difficult to come to terms with.

Even though I *know* I had no choice—I *know* I was an innocent child—the guilt is so strong.

Of course, this was the network's attempt to make me into one of them. How else do they keep the organisation strong if they don't recruit from within their own ranks.

And who better to recruit than children who are already broken mentally and emotionally.

It also made me *complicit.*

How could I ever report what was happening if I was one of them — if I was guilty of their crimes.

In retrospect, with my trauma-aware adult brain in place, it's *obvious* it wasn't my fault. But try explaining that to an eight-year-old. Or more accurately... try *expecting* an eight-year-old to figure that out on their own. It's not going to happen.

Talking 'complicit', Sarah's story takes things to the next level.

It's the same knife and the same man as the opening flashback. Still Melissa. But this time *my hands* are holding the knife. And his hands are wrapped firmly around mine.

I had no choice. He was way stronger than me. Wherever he directed the knife, it went. But technically, I was the one holding it. *Technically.*

You see where this is going?

There was a victim strapped to the board. The same board that Eve's victims were strapped to. The same one *I'd* been strapped to in some of Rachel's flashbacks.

He pointed the knife at my belly and gave me the choice... either I die right now, or we go through with it. It? I wasn't sure exactly what 'it' was...

But I resisted and stopped the knife from pressing any harder into my belly.

The choice was made.

Some fucking choice, right?

But you see what they did? Very clever. Now whatever happened next was *my* fault. I'd had fair warning.

I'd made my 'choice'.

Melissa handed over to Sarah at that point.

She *knew* what happened, but didn't get any sight, sound or feelings from it to begin with.

And when she handed back to Melissa, it was all done.

There was a simple word from the man:

"You're one of us now. You can never tell anyone."

I'm not going to talk in depth about what Sarah saw, or did. But believe me, she was *so* reluctant to even show *me.*

She would show me the motion of our hands, but not give any visuals.

She kept doing this. Over and over re-enacting the exact motions. I knew *exactly* what she was doing.

And she kept trying to re-enact it physically too. On me.

I honestly had to hide the sharp knives in the house for a good few weeks, cooking my Bolognese sauce by cutting the vegetables with a table knife. It came out surprisingly good with its 'rustic' veg.

Eventually I knew this had to stop—she had to let it out *somehow*—so I left the coloured pencils and sketch book out on the kitchen table once again.

A day or so later, she sat down to draw.

I can see her picture now in my mind. I don't want to, but I don't think it's something you unsee once you've seen it. Detailed. Anatomical. Awful.

She began to bring me clearer and clearer visuals over the coming days and weeks. I almost wished she didn't, but I knew she had to let it out. So I continued to love her. I continued to affirm her. And I continued to drum it home that she's safe now, and not in that room.

But for all the visuals and bodily motions I'd been shown, something was missing.

The feelings.

Of course they were.

How could anyone *possibly* carry the feelings of what she had done? Impossible. Not if you wanted to survive.

It was one day short of a month after Sarah emerged that Ruth finally showed herself. *She* carried the feelings. And holy fucking shit, what a lot of feelings there were.

I'm not even going there...

Suffice to say the groceries didn't get bought that day. I didn't go to my acoustic club that evening. I wasn't functional for several days.

The most horrific feelings, bottled for decades?

They mature. They ferment. They get a special level of spicy.

❧

It took such a long time, and a lot of therapy hours to come to terms with what Sarah and Ruth brought to me. Of course the whole scenario was *designed* to be irreconcilable. It's what broke me fully. It's what made Melissa so terrified to disobey — she knew the consequences.

And, as the man said, it made me one of *them.*

Except it didn't. Because I knew *deep down* that I was *never* one of them. I still knew right from wrong. I knew good from evil. No matter how hard they tried, they couldn't break my soul.

I honestly don't know how.

I have no idea how I turned out loving, compassionate and soft after everything I've been through.

But I did.

And I am grateful for that.

So, so grateful.

# 20. Kill-Switch

I was holed up under my desk, screaming into my plushie. I don't know how long I'd been there... twenty minutes? Maybe thirty? If you've done any disciplined mindfulness practice—and I had: about fifteen years' worth—you know that thoughts are like the weather, they pass. You know that thoughts are not 'truth', they are merely suggestions.

But these thoughts were different. They just *wouldn't* pass.

The voice was so clear: "*End it now.*"

When I wrote my song—*Inconvenience*—about surviving the 'kill-switch' I included the line I literally spoke out loud while I was under the desk. Sobbing into my plushie, struggling to catch my breath, I quietly murmured to myself:

> "*I think they might still win this time*
> *I think I might destroy me.*"

Thankfully, as with every time the kill-switch has triggered—*spoiler alert: I'm still here*—I managed to get through it. I honestly don't know how. Maybe luck. Maybe pure bloody-mindedness. Maybe invoking the mantra that so many survivors of ritual abuse carry: "I'm going to survive out of *spite,* if nothing else!"

But honestly, as I read through this manuscript in the editing process, and I read those two lines? The emotional dam burst. *Truly* burst. I was bawling into my pillow. Emotionally I was back there under the desk.

Those moments spent under the desk, terrified, with that clear instruction in my head was definitely the closest I've ever been to the abyss, and I'd rather not go back there again.

Ever.

❧

The kill switch it brutal. It's precise. It's emotionless.

It is simply an instruction: "End it now."

It is a protection mechanism designed by the networks to prevent their victims from getting anywhere close to being a threat.

You find joy in life and begin to thrive? Fire the kill-switch.

You start to find success and manage to sustain yourself independently? Fire the kill-switch.

You start to tell the truth about what happened? Holy fuck... fire the kill-switch and *keep pressing that fucking button until it works.*

It's a relentless onslaught. And if it doesn't make you actually end it, it's designed to drive you crazy. Again, the lyrics from "Inconvenience" tell the story:

> *She wasn't meant to make it out,*
> *was meant to fade in silence,*
> *bottle, blade or padded room,*
> *whichever came the fastest.*

I experienced that relentless triggering for a few months as I went deeper and deeper into the abuse. Two or three times a week, the voice would come. Clear. Authoritative. Impossible —in theory—to disobey.

I've spoken with other survivors who have experienced the same. The methods are often creative, but they're always very precise.

I was waiting for my best friend to arrive for climbing one morning and the voice spoke:

> *"Transfer all your money to your friend. Leave the front door ajar so she can get in. Go to the downstairs bathroom. End it. And make it tidy."*

I think it was during this particular incident that I *truly* realised this was programming. You see, suicidal thoughts *should* come with emotion. Maybe despondency. Hopelessness. Depression, perhaps?

Or if not strong emotion, they should come with a distinct *lack* of emotion: a deep *numbness.*

Suicidal thoughts should not come at 9:43am when you've just got out of the shower, and you're deciding which t shirt to put on to go climbing...

"The cute cat one? Or the one with the puppy? Or maybe... yeah, I should probably kill myself."

Hmm... decisions... cat? dog? death?

While the kill-switch became particularly active during my recovery—not surprising, since I had started telling the truth, and saying it out loud—it *had* triggered before, much earlier in my life...

The first time I remember was some thirty-odd years ago, when I was living independently for the first time. I had gone to university and completed my first year. My mother had rented our family home out and gone travelling. And so I stayed in my university city for the summer.

I found somewhere to stay, got a job, and was really finding my feet, *following my natural rhythms,* as my therapist likes to encourage me to do even now.

I still had access to the campus and had been there doing some off-curriculum work. I'd finished up and was cycling back to my digs. I clearly remember the spot. The quiet road, alongside the sports field. The birds flitting in the hedgerow. The oncoming bus.

And the voice: "Swerve in front of the bus. Now."

Thankfully I didn't. But it shook me for sure.

I honestly didn't think much of it after the fact. Weird incident. Nothing bad happened. Move on.

❧

The next time I clearly remember the kill switch was an altogether more distressing event. But it was also a life-changing liberation.

I was *much* more serious about going through with it this time.

It was 2018, and I was the most successful I had ever been in my business and finances. I was earning good money. I was famous in my niche. Published. Taking regular speaking engagements. And kinda loving life.

But the voice came, and it was relentless.

It was the middle of the night and I took myself for a long walk to distract myself and get some thinking room.

I realised a couple of things...

Firstly, it wasn't necessarily trying to kill *me.* It was only trying to kill my *success.* I realised that if I would shrink back and make myself invisible again, the voice would be satisfied.

That is, ultimately, what I chose to do. I dropped my clients, closed the business, and started struggling financially again — taking up vital mental space that might have been used to uncover the abuse.

But I also realised something else:

If I was willing to end it, then I was also *free to live my life however I wanted.* I could blow the biggest raspberry to expectations, to society, to family tradition and honestly do what the fuck I wanted in whichever *way* I wanted. I realised that if it all went south—if I ended up starving to death in an alcoholic haze on a park bench—then it was *still* better than not being here, and if it all got too much I could always carry out the original plan anyway.

I still believe that is the *best* antidote to suicide, whether led by programming or despondency — it paradoxically gives you freedom. Gives you *choice.*

So I'd had the epiphany. And it's exactly what I did.

I started living my life for me.

I said 'fuck it' to so many aspects of life.

I said 'no' when I wanted to say 'no'. I learnt about boundaries. I learnt about self-advocacy. And as I've already discussed, I learnt that my mother was an emotionally abusive, boundary-crushing narcissist.

The seeds for *my whole fucking life* were sown that night.

I had no idea of the impact of the decision to live unapologetically, but it set off such a profound sequence of events...

As we know, I cut off my mother. That gave me the space to question my relationship. That gave me the motivation to divorce (as mentioned before, we are still great friends). That gave me the space to breathe, and ultimately *that* gave me the safety to uncover the abuse...

Ironically, the kill-switch that was meant to destroy me and protect the network actually led to their total exposure.

Sorry guys — you failed...

*I am your inconvenience,*
*The one you meant to lose,*
*The silence you invested in,*
*The one who slipped the noose.*
*I speak with all the names you stole,*
*I burn what you controlled.*
*You tried to make me disappear,*
*But I never lost my soul.*

***— from "Inconvenience" by Georgia Snow***

*https://georgiasnow.bandcamp.com/track/inconvenience*

# 21. Katie

*I was lying in bed and he just walked in.*

*Naked. Ready.*

*I rolled my eyes, let out a quiet, whispered sigh, and got in position.*

When this flashback appeared, I was confused. I couldn't figure out which girl it was. It had a hint of Chloe about it, but it wasn't her. It didn't add up.

But it continued:

*As he went about his business, I crossed my right arm over in front of me and rested my head on it. My left? I sucked my thumb for comfort.*

I was still so confused. *Was* it Chloe? Was it an older part of Chloe? Maybe it was Laura, but her experiences were in hotel rooms with strangers. This was at home. And he was certainly no stranger.

*When he was done he just kinda wandered off.*

*I rolled onto my side in a foetal position and lay there feeling totally worthless and depressed.*

I mostly came out of the flashback, but stayed in that foetal position for about thirty minutes. I knew that I had chores to do — I needed to get up and fetch some groceries at least.

But whenever I sent the 'come on, girl... get up now' signal to my muscles, they would twitch slightly but deliver nothing more than that.

It took the longest time for my physical body to come back online and actually move, so deep was the 'freeze' response.

And this isn't rare. Many women—even in long-term relationships and marriages—find themselves enduring sex they don't want, simply to appease a partner's entitlement. I once read a man write, "I guess lying on your back for five minutes twice a week to have a happy marriage isn't worth it to a lot of women."

As if our bodies are maintenance tools. As if our consent is a chore to be managed.

This kind of violation doesn't always come with violence or threats. Sometimes it comes with obligation. With resignation. With silence.

And that's what made this flashback so chilling. It wasn't fear. It was obedience.

❧

It was later in the day that clarity began emerging.

As it does with so many parts, it came in small realisations. In fragments.

Firstly some speculation:

> *It was weird that he just stood there and expected me to know what to do. And I did it... and I was,*

*like, so resigned... Just reluctantly going through the motions...*

*The surrogate spouse?*

Survivors of incest have often not heard the phrase 'surrogate spouse', but when they do, everything suddenly falls into place. It's that dynamic where a parent substitutes their child into the roles their spouse should fulfil — whether that's practical, emotional or sexual.

Even later, more clarity came. My heart was getting heavier:

*Okay... Shit this is big.*

*This is 14 or 15 years old.*

Then she simply gave me her name:

*Samantha*

I realised that my response to his approach had been the typical response you'd expect from a surly teen who was basically 'done with this shit'.

But the worst part? I'd always believed the abuse had ended when my father left — when I was eleven.

This changed everything.

The shifting horizon of my abuse was such a difficult thing to process each time it moved. I first thought the abuse was *very* short-term, around the age of three. Maybe an isolated incident or two.

All of my recovered memories had been in the house I lived in from birth. And some time before my fourth birthday we'd had a fire and subsequently moved to a new place.

My optimistic mind wrapped up the entire mystery... he burnt the house down to destroy the evidence and the abuse stopped. Done. Clean. *Just about* palatable if you're being generous.

But then I realised the significance of the *blanks* I talked about in chapter four. It had gone on into the next house. Until the age of eleven. That's when my father left. And I stopped wetting the bed. And... well, obviously it ended then.

Of course, Chloe then revealed it all began at birth. That was a tough one for sure.

But Samantha? Fifteen?

Shouldn't I have *said* something? Shouldn't I have *stopped* him? Shouldn't I have *noticed it was wrong and told someone?*

Honestly, these are the struggles that survivors face every single fucking day.

Those questions are *so* common from survivors of *all sorts* of sexual assault.

If only I'd said 'no' harder. If only I hadn't gone round in the first place. If only... If only...

We drive ourselves crazy.

*Why* didn't I do something differently?

And you know what? The answer is *always* the same. This is the truth that we are talked out of, either by ourselves or by the systems that protect abusers...

Every survivor needs to know this:

> It wasn't your fault.
> *Nothing* you did, or didn't do, caused the abuse.
> The *perpetrator's choices* caused the abuse.

Even when I told my best friend—who had accepted, after a shaky start, that abuse was real—she said "Fifteen? No. You would've remembered."

I couldn't knock her logic. Of *course* I would've remembered. That is if my mind hadn't already been programmed for years to a) comply, and b) dissociate.

❧

Samantha presented another important issue that survivors struggle with:

Is it rape if I willingly presented myself to him?

This is *such* a heavy question to deal with, and believe me it led to a whole rabbit-hole of research about consent.

The answer, of course, is *yes, it is rape.*

But why?

Well, for starters, a minor can't consent. Clear. Simple.

But for those who aren't minors?

Well, the best description I've heard for consent is:

> *Consent is an* enthusiastic *and* ongoing *'yes'.*
> *Anything else is a 'no'.*

This covers all those 'blurred lines'—ugh—of people who consented then passed out, those who consented to one activity, but then boundaries started getting crossed. It covers those who are enthusiastic but then become unsure or hesitant. And it covers those who were coerced into their 'yes'. Every single one of those cases is a 'no'.

We're taught that 'no means no', but we're not taught that 'maybe' means 'no' and 'um...' means 'no' and 'can you hold on a minute...' means 'no'.

Incidentally, France, at the time of writing, has just updated its rape laws[15] after the high-profile case of Gisèle Pelicot whose husband drugged her, then invited men to come round and rape her while she was unconscious.

The perpetrators tried to defend themselves by saying that they didn't know she was not in a position to give consent. Yeah. Maybe a legal loophole, but holy hell. The lengths some men will go to in order to excuse their behaviour.

This ruling is a *huge* victory for women. French law now says that consent must be "free and informed, specific, prior and revocable". And, importantly, silence or lack of response does *not* constitute consent.

15 Gozzi, L. (2025). France enshrines need for consent into rape law in wake of Gisèle Pelicot case. BBC News. [online] 29 Oct. Available at: https://www.bbc.co.uk/news/articles/ce9d3ldgg5vo.

The rest of the world may not be so progressive, but the principle still stands:

A man getting to satisfy his desires *never* overrides a woman's dignity, safety, or wishes. And let's be real, men will frame it as *need,* but when it comes down to it, it's *desire.*

Men *desire* to have sex. Women *need* dignity and safety.

I know men are fragile. But a man's disappointment, mild ego-bruising, and blue balls *do not* excuse a woman's harm or violation. Ever.

I'll say it again: if it isn't an enthusiastic and ongoing 'yes', then it is a 'no'. And 'no' means stop.

Samantha's flashbacks didn't go on for too long. She was soon followed up by Katie.

Katie was *clearly* the *same girl* as Samantha, but with a different experience. That happens often. It happened with Debbie's fear and Fiona's performance. Same with Laura's pleasing and Andrea's punishment. Twin parts.

Where Samantha had rolled her eyes and reluctantly submitted to the violation, Katie opened a whole new world to me. A whole new dimension of confusion and shame.

I talked about the benefits of logging every flashback when we were meeting Debbie. How, when things are difficult to revisit, I can simply retrieve my flashback report from the archive.

I think I'm going to do the same here. I'll share exactly what I wrote the first time Katie emerged:

> *Oh god... I don't even know how to talk about this.*
>
> *I think it was a flashback... hard to say.*
>
> *I was actually just relaxing in bed, having a bit of "me time" with my magic wand.*

No shame, right? Honestly, I wish I'd discovered the magic wand earlier in life.

I digress...

> *Suddenly I found myself getting into position in knees and elbows, presenting myself, and I said out loud, before I realised it, "Come on, daddy... fuck me, daddy..."*
>
> *Ugh. I came to orgasm with that in my throat...*
>
> *Ugh.*
>
> *And I wasn't being figurative.*
>
> *Ugh.*
>
> *Was this a flashback. Did that happen?*
>
> *No other reason to perform it now, right?*
>
> *Ugh.*

Shit, right? The disgust is apparent.

It got worse.

Where Samantha lay there afterwards, frozen, questioning life itself? Katie lay there with a warm glow. Satisfaction. Feeling *loved.*

She...

Can I even say it?

She fucking *enjoyed* it.

This is *exactly* the situation where we find what we're made of — where we discover if our survivor toolkit is truly up to scratch. Whether we can cut it with the *difficult* parts.

Because holy hell.

The *correct* response to a part emerging is to accept her. Love her. Witness her. Don't flinch. Tell her it wasn't her fault.

But a fifteen-year-old? Inviting it? *Seducing* him? And then enjoying every moment of it?

That is challenging to love unless you've already had practice.

This is the point in many survivors' stories where I read the words "I hate myself. I'm so disgusting. I hate Katie."

You really have to grit your teeth. Ground yourself.

And simply say:

> "Katie. I see you. I love you. This wasn't your fault. The pleasure just proved that your body was working properly. I know you didn't want this. You were groomed. You are not to blame. You were *never* to blame. You are not disgusting. I love you and you are safe now."

You sit with her. Even while she's telling you—you, her *mother*—what a wonderful man she's met.

You bite your tongue.

But what you also do is go fucking *full-on mama bear* for her. And that's what I did next.

Katie's flashbacks were increasing in frequency. She was verbalising everything she said to him at the time. She was enjoying every minute, and lying there in the warm glow of someone who is truly loved.

I would feel a flashback coming on, and—oh my god, it pains me to admit this—shamefully lean *in* to it because they were so pleasurable.

I've said it before. I'll say it again — Ugh.

But even this truly fucked-up idyll wasn't all rosy.

I mean, for starters, she was fucking her father. But she was also naïve. He would scoot out of the room straight afterwards *every time.* She didn't receive any *actual* love, care or attention.

And she would call out a quiet, tragic "thank you" to the open doorway that he had disappeared through.

She was glowing, but empty.

But also coming back for more. And more.

That's when I stepped in.

It was 3:40 in the morning, early October. I was having an all-too-common disturbed night, and I was *just* starting to drop off to sleep again.

Katie came back, and *he* was there hovering next to the bed expectantly.

Big Georgia stepped in. Me. Adult me.

I'm not sure how it worked... was it part of the flashback? Did I hijack it and insert myself into the scene?

It didn't matter. There I was...

"NO! She's *not* going to invite you in, you monster."

This was re-parenting at its finest.

Where the child part can't or doesn't know to do the right thing, the adult-self can step in and either *guide* them, or as in this case, *protect* them.

This was wholly new to me. I've visualised rescue scenarios before, but this was the first time I'd stepped into one, live, in real-time.

"You fucking abusive asshole, taking advantage of a young girl like that. Your own daughter."

I flipped my middle finger at him.

"*I'm* protecting her now and *you* no longer have access."

Katie had thought she knew what love was. But her view was skewed by grooming and conditioning. Now she saw it for real. Someone *actually* standing up for her. Someone who *actually* cared for her safety and wellbeing.

She felt happier now than the abuse ever made her feel.

She felt seen. She felt protected.

Dare I say, loved?

I was still *fiercely* standing my ground.

"No! Fuck off. You are a *monster.* Fuck. Off."

I am *just* as passionate about calling out abusers as I am about protecting victims. It all comes from the same value, really — a deep desire for *justice.* And I will fight for that justice with love *and* fire.

I think maybe Katie had kept showing me what she went through because this is exactly what she needed — she needed someone—*me*—to step in for her.

Remember what Clare saw? Remember how Laura had been created? What Sarah was forced to participate in?

Katie was the fifteen-year-old product of all that deliberate programming, reinforcement, coercion and—let's call it what it is—mind-fuckery.

Her invitations were a *survival* mechanism. Don't disobey. Get it over with as quickly as possible.

Her pleasure was a *coping* mechanism. While I'm here, and can't get away, I might as well at least enjoy it.

All survival, really.

'Coping' is just the emotional and mental part of survival.

None of her behaviour was authentic. None of it was desired.

And she was never to blame.

❧

In my survivors' forum, I was talking about Katie and Samantha — and Louise, a related part who took on things I won't speak about here. I was grieving the fact that the abuse continued until *at least* the age of fifteen.

Do you feel it?

Do you feel those sneaky little words loitering menacingly there in the darkness?

At least?

Oh crap.

By now, twenty-eight parts under my belt, I just went in directly and asked.

"Georgia... when was the last time your dad raped you?"

She—I, really—didn't even take very long to reply.

"Twenty four."

"Okay. Thank you. I love you."

I didn't pry. I knew I didn't need to. When she was ready, she'd come and show herself.

❧

Charlotte appeared a day or two after I asked the question.

Twenty-four.

Twenty-fucking-four.

If you thought I should have remembered what happened at fifteen? Well *surely* I could remember twenty-four?

I could. Not the abuse, obviously. But I remember swinging by a fetish fair to pick up supplies on the way to visit my father one time. Literally buying the equipment—collar, cuffs, gag—for him to abuse me with.

I didn't know that's why I was buying it at the time. But it always kinda bugged me why I would buy it on the way *to* his house, and not after I'd visited.

And consent? Saying no?

A grown adult?

If you thought I should have said 'no' at fifteen? Surely... *surely* I knew to say 'no' at twenty-four?

It seems not.

Twenty four was coincidentally the last time I visited my father alone for decades. I found a partner around then and only visited as part of a couple after that. Probably not a coincidence, right?

❧

With Charlotte, you've now met all the parts who split to protect me. There are a couple of very special parts still to come — but they're different in nature, entirely.

As I edit this manuscript, I realise the emotional connection to these parts is sometimes lacking — they feel a little *detached.*

As I mentioned in Rachel's chapter, you might sometimes feel like you're reading a work of fiction, not an account of real events that happened to a real girl — me.

If you've found yourself feeling that, then you now know *exactly* how dissociation works — and how it protects you.

Because of the dissociation—the splitting—I even *experienced* many of these events as a kind of fiction. As someone else.

That's the true genius of the mind's protective mechanisms in the face of unthinkable, unbearable suffering.

It's all very real. But if you can just compartmentalise it—keep it *'over there'* in a neat little package like Rachel, or Laura, or Charlotte—then it becomes bearable.

❧

With Katie, I felt like I had finally done the thing so many survivors struggle to do: I had stood up for the part who felt the most difficult, the most unlovable.

The part whose mind had been twisted into thinking her abuse was affection.

The part whose survival meant seduction.

The part whose 'yes' was never a real yes.

I thought that would be the end of it. But of course it wasn't. Because what followed her wasn't another girl.

It was the feeling she left behind.

*Shame.*

# 22. Shame

*Keep quiet. Don't talk about it. Don't upset people.*

This is the message that lives in survivors' bones. It's placed there by abusers and by society alike.

Abusers have an *incredible* knack for making children think it's *their* fault they are being abused. This was something that hit me when I first opened Penny Parks' book[16], even before I recovered any memories.

Just three paragraphs into the book, on line twenty-five of the introduction, Parks says:

> *The aggressor capitalises on the child's naïvety and threatens that the child will 'be in trouble', 'go to jail', 'not be loved anymore' or perhaps 'have to go away' if she tells anyone about what she—the child—has done.*

Holy crap.

*Go to jail?*

Within *forty-three seconds* of opening this book, I knew it was for me.

---

16 'Rescuing The Inner Child', as mentioned in Vanessa's chapter, was my portal to revealing the abuse.

All my life I'd had this feeling in the back of my mind that I would, at some point, go to jail for some as-yet-unspecified crime.

Honestly. I thought it was the default. I thought basically *everyone* went to jail at least once in their life.

I'd never really thought too deeply about it. Nor thought it was weird. As the evidence mounted that I *hadn't* actually gone to jail yet, I guess the thoughts subsided over time.

But the moment I read that line?

Shit. She *sees* me.

Now, you might say this was *guilt,* and you'd be right to an extent. It *starts* as a feeling of guilt, but over time, with enough repetition, guilt turns to shame.

Guilt says 'I *made* a mistake.' Shame gives the altogether more soul-destroying message — 'I *am* a mistake.'

You can fix guilt.

*Authentic* guilt—the sort you experience when you have *actually done something wrong*—can be fixed easily. You just need to make amends.

It's so simple.

You break someone's favourite mug? You replace it.

You say harsh words you regret? You apologise.

*Neurotic* guilt is another matter. This is the sort of guilt you feel when you *haven't* actually done anything wrong, but someone has decided that you have — maybe setting a very reasonable boundary. Or telling the truth.

This is the kind of guilt we internalise from dysfunctional families, teachers and other institutions.

And it can't be fixed with amends because there are no amends to be made. The only way you can fix it—or *believe* you can fix it—is through *punishment.*

I swear, there's a tremendous industry built around punishing men for their neurotic guilt. It makes them feel better in the moment, but because it doesn't fix anything, they keep coming back and paying the dominatrices to beat them and berate them (I mentioned—in chapter nineteen—that I had considered sex work, right? This type had been firmly on the shortlist. I knew there was a willing market.)

But that's *guilt.* And we're not here to talk about guilt.

What of *shame?*

❧

Shame goes so much deeper than guilt. Shame is the killer. There is no solution. No amends to be made. No punishment that can 'fix' it.

You *are* a mistake.

Even the darkest, most sordid degradation doesn't make that better because it's your *identity,* not your behaviour.

And that's how I felt for most of my life.

"I am worthless. I am flawed. I am a burden."

I even carried my shame from birth. My mother went to great pains to explain to me, whenever she could, that I sat on her sciatic nerve when she was pregnant with me, and she hated me for it.

Then I came late.

And when I was born, I was huge.

In adulthood I hadn't really remembered those messages she drummed into me in childhood... but I did always panic about being late. And think I was fat. I mean, I *am* fat but that's not the point hre — that's likely identity *leading* behaviour and habits.

I also knew that I got on everyone's nerves.

Shame. All shame.

The belief: I was *born* horribly flawed and there was nothing I could do about it.

❧

Of course, the abusers do everything they can to *instill* shame. It's probably the best way to keep a child small, insecure, compliant and needy. When you destroy their very identity, they will do anything for *any* scrap of validation. Anything to tell them they might just be okay. Or at least tolerable. Or useful.

And once the shame is in the bones, it's almost impossible to shift without a *lot* of therapy and a *lot* of self-love.

The number of times I see survivors in support groups saying "I feel so disgusting and shameful" is tragic. *Truly* tragic.

They haven't shifted their shame yet. They need to realise it was *never* their fault. They need to realise—and internalise—they they are perfect and lovable *exactly* as they are.

I was trapped in shame for years and years. Thankfully I read *many* books on the subject and my relationship with shame had become pretty healthy by the time the abuse emerged. I think that contributed a great deal to the speed at which I was able to process what happened.

I particularly found John Bradshaw and David R. Hawkins[17] helpful. They approached the subject from completely different angles, clinical and spiritual respectively.

As I read Bradshaw's *'Healing the Shame That Binds You*[18]*,'* I got a great deal from it. But I also recognised so many of the symptoms of shame in my mother. I lent her the book. She returned it not long after, unread. She wasn't ready to face her shame, and continued projecting it onto others, including me.

17 Start with Hawkins D.R. (2015). Transcending the levels of consciousness : the stairway to enlightenment. Carlsbad, California: Hay House, Inc.

18 Bradshaw, J. (2005). Healing the Shame That Binds You. Deerfield Beach, Florida: Health Communications, Inc.

That's not uncommon. It takes a tremendous amount of courage and vulnerability to face your shame. A *tremendous* amount.

Talking about projection...

That's *such* an important point... Many people try to say there is no shame in abuse. And they're wrong. They're, handing the victim well-meaning platitudes, but they're *minimising* the problem.

There is a *lot* of shame around abuse. A metric fuckton of it, if we're going to be real. But the key for the victim is that *none of the shame rests on their shoulders.* Or none of it *should,* anyway.

Abusers tend to be *filled* with deep shame. And like bigots, religious fanatics and fascists, they *project* their shame out in to the world. They carry such deep, unresolved shame that they can't help but harm and control others in order to try to feel better. Of course, they don't *actually* feel better, so they double-down on the harm.

If they would just face themselves in the mirror, and get some therapy, I swear the world would be a *much* better place.

But back to the shame of abuse and where it rests...

It was only when I let go of the shame of my re-enactments that my girls would come to me and talk about it.

Shame makes you shrink. Shame makes you silent. Shame makes you hide.

The abusers transfer the shame onto your shoulders and you feel so worthless that you don't even *realise* you can talk to anyone about it. You must have done something wrong. You must be flawed.

Shame makes you *isolate.* If anyone knew the *real you,* they would discover how unlovable you are.

Those are the lies that shame tells us.

The antidote?

Talking about it.

That's what I'm doing in this book.

Loudly, unapologetically *talking about it.*

It's what I do in my songs. It's what I do in my workshops.

I've been referred to as *'the woman who survived abuse and won't shut the fuck up about it.'* I see that as a badge of honour.

Shame loves secrecy. Shame loves silence. And if you just begin to talk—anonymously if you need to, perhaps in an online support group; or with a trusted professional like a therapist; or with a trusted friend (if you can *truly* trust them)—you will find that the shame will lift. Slowly to begin with. But with increasing momentum. And a liberating sense of empowerment.

That's exactly what I found.

For years I did my healing solo. I couldn't trust *anyone.* I watched YouTube videos on narcissistic parents, and boundaries. And I pored through my 'recovery bible'—Pete Walker's *Complex PTSD: From Surviving To Thriving*[19]—until I could get to a point where I could trust another human.

I should point out that the 'solo phase' is *perfectly* valid, and absolutely necessary for many survivors. Relational healing—involving other people—can come later once the nervous system has begun to believe it can trust.

When I started working with my therapist it was *deeply* uncomfortable. And not because she was a bad therapist. No, it was the opposite. It's because she was—and is—a *brilliant* therapist.

I tentatively talked about a couple of slightly shameful aspects of my life. A little tester. And she just accepted them. Like... *just accepted them.* It was so alien after living a life of scrutiny, judgement and shame.

I literally walked into my third therapy session—having been thinking about this 'problem' on the walk to her place—addressed her assertively by her first name, and said, "Would you *please stop* being so *fucking accepting.*" I was only half-joking.

19 Walker, P. (2013). Complex PTSD: From Surviving to Thriving: A Guide and Map for Recovering from Childhood Trauma. Lafayette, Ca: Azure Coyote.

She had absolutely perfected the formula for destroying shame — create an environment where your clients feel safe to talk about what they find shameful.

And the first step is to accept what your clients say without judgement, and with—as they say in therapy circles—*unconditional positive regard.*

It's so simple and so effective.

She didn't need to fix me. I could do that myself. I just needed to be *heard* without judgement.

❧

Prior to understanding shame my life was a mess.

I spent most of my life bleeding out on jobs while not asking for appropriate compensation. Without standing my ground. on crossed boundaries and unreasonable demands.

My god.

I was also re-enacting so much of my abuse.

I covered this in the 'Fetishes' chapter, but I would be indulging in all sorts of fetish behaviour which *should* be exploratory, or fun. But because of the shame it was just miserable. Dark, miserable and lonely.

I couldn't even share it with partners. That might have made it more palatable. Or fun. But the shame kept me silent — and isolated in my pain.

It wasn't just lonely, it was also so *expensive* with the frequently discarded and replaced kit. Again, all shame-driven.

And all the while I didn't think I was worthy of help. Or of friendship. Or connection. Or anything, really.

That's how shame affects you. Deeply and disturbingly.

❧

So that's *personal* shame, but what of *societal* shame and *institutional* shame.

It's very similar.

It says *'that's too much'*. It says *'stay small'*, *'don't make people uncomfortable'*, *'stay silent.'*

And it causes *so much harm.*

It prevents survivors from ever coming forward. They know that they will be disbelieved. Minimised. Questioned.

The shame of society would rather brush abuse under the carpet than admit it really happens.

This was one of the biggest lessons early on in my healing.

I *knew* it couldn't be real because abuse doesn't really happen, does it?

I mean, it happens in the news, and in dramas, sure. But not in *my* town. Not in *my* street. Certainly not in *my* living room.

Honestly the biggest obstacle in getting anyone to believe that abuse happened to you? Getting them to believe abuse really happens *at all.*

Society just doesn't want it to be true.

This is where we get back to the problems I had with my early parts. I believed *them,* but I didn't believe *it.*

The truth is that abusers don't need to be *smart* — they just need to be *bold.* Society will do the work for them by refusing to engage with something so horrific. Too shameful. Not going there.

I believe this is changing, with the #MeToo movement, with the Jeffrey Epstein case, with Virginia Giuffre's testimony[20], with other survivors speaking out loud.

But this movement is being *driven.* It needs constant effort. Especially since there are a lot of powerful white men in suits who are *very* willing to manipulate society to look the other way to protect their friends.

Leave it to the patriarchy to set the standards, and abuse will vanish again into obscurity. It won't stop happening, but it will slip out of the public consciousness again, and even out of credibility. It will become all-too-easily deniable again.

20 Giuffre, V. (2025). Nobody's Girl: A Memoir of Surviving Abuse and Fighting for Justice. 1st ed. Doubleday.

Even in what should be the safest spaces, shame can sometimes be used to silence survivors...

In one survivors' space I was a member of, I gently challenged a man who was looking for signals of romantic interest from women half his age who were simply being polite as part of their job.

Over time, as it became clear he was ignoring feedback and doubling down, I spoke more directly. That's how I roll.

The moderators hid my replies and defended his right to 'ask questions,' even as the questions reeked of boundary-blurring entitlement.

I was told I was 'not the person they knew,' as though speaking plainly about predatory behaviour somehow disqualified my entire presence as a survivor.

The reason I was 'not the person they knew' is because, up to that point, they had only seen me support survivors — never confront a threat.

They hadn't seen the 'me' that is equally passionate about calling out wrong as it is about supporting the vulnerable.

As I mentioned before, these are both simply expressions of my fierce passion for justice. And maybe my *extremely* low tolerance for bullshit.

This is what survivor shame looks like in the wild. This is how we are told, again and again, that it is better to be polite than to be truthful. That it's better to let the predator feel safe than to name danger when we see it.

This is why shame is sometimes *so* hard to shake. Even in supposedly safe spaces, sometimes when you finally dare to speak, the world answers with a firm *"Shhh."*

❧

If you carry shame, please know — it was *never yours to carry.* You were *never* the problem.

And when you're ready to lay it down, you won't be alone.

Many of us are refusing to stay silent.

We are naming shame for what it is — a tool of the abuser, and a failure of society.

And once it's named, it loses its power.

This is how we heal. *Out loud.*

# 23. Peach

I was six years old. In the box. I'm not sure if Amanda had split yet, but I was ready to give up.

I could feel my soul being drained by the second.

This is it, I thought. This is where it ends.

But there was something inside me. That spark. That tiny speck of light that shines as bright as a thousand suns.

It was still there, but I could see it starting to fade.

I don't know how I knew to do this, but this little girl, the six-year-old fucking *genius* got to work on her psyche.

She took the spark and wrapped it as tightly as she could.

Newspaper, bandages, blankets, tape — whatever she could find in the recesses of her mind. And she wrapped that spark as tightly as she could so not even the faintest glimmer would give it away.

Then she buried it. Deep. So deep that *whatever happened to her*—no matter what evils those men came up with—they would *never* reach the spark.

It never ceases to amaze me what a human being in survival mode is capable of. Even at the age of six.

She—I—had done a great job.

It took *decades* to even realise the spark was there.

Of course, the spark was another dissociated part, who would be known as Peach, but I didn't know that at the time.

She tried to come out a few times through my life, but my environment just wasn't set up for her.

I used to say I wasn't creative — that I didn't have an artistic bone in my body. And honestly, I believed it.

But every time Peach tried to show her colours—her imagination, her chaos, her joy—she was met with *shame.* My parents didn't just ignore her, they peed on her tentative little parade:

> *"What are you doing that for?"*
> *"Stop wasting your time with that silliness..."*
> *"That's a nice picture, pass me the pencil..."*

Creativity was *bad.* Creativity was *embarrassing.* Creativity was *'too much.'*

Honestly, she didn't stand a fucking chance.

So I left her buried. She was buried so deep, and for so long that I totally forgot she was even there.

But come on — I've written books. Built businesses. Composed and produced songs. Good songs, even if I say so myself.

Not creative? *Bullshit.*

Peach has always been here. I was just taught to be *afraid* of her, just as my parents were afraid of *me.*

When your world revolves around *control,* creativity is *deeply* dangerous.

So some thirty-two years after the bulk of the abuse ended, I found her one day. A tiny glimmer in the darkness of my soul, and believe me, my soul was an *incredibly* dark place at that time.

But there she was. A glimmer.

Without even knowing what it was, I began peeling back the layers protecting it. Arduous work. Damn, I had wrapped it up well.

I could *see* its brightness, even if I couldn't access it.

I wrote, *at the time,* about the light that burns with the brightness of a thousand suns trapped within us. I didn't realise this was a personal experience, I think I projected it onto the world and assumed everyone had the same experience. Maybe they do to some extent — books like The Artists Way[21] wouldn't need to exist if there weren't a *lot* of people with their light wrapped up.

Of course, I had no idea that most people *hadn't* had to dissociate to survive, and that I *had.*

I kept going.

---

21 Cameron, J. (2021). The Artists Way: A Spiritual Path to Higher Creativity. Uk: Profile Books Ltd.

I recognised my 'inner child' in the spark, and learnt how to communicate with her. I called her 'Georgia the Innocent'. Remember, at this time, I still had my birth name... it would be *years* before I would change my name to erase the abusers and finally honour my inner child. I didn't name her after me, I named *me* after *her.*

Incidentally, my middle name—Alison—is in honour of Alison Clarkson, better known as Betty Boo *(Doin' the Do)*, a joyful, unapologetic lighthouse of hope and rap-pop for me during my mid-to-late teens. I perform a few of her songs at acoustic nights and folk clubs, and they always go down well.

I'm usually the first—and only—person who has ever performed a Betty Boo song at any particular folk club.

❧

So my relationship with my inner child slowly grew. Not with *deep* levels of trust, but with enough to converse, and for me to understand some of her needs.

The breakthrough came, though, in early 2025 when I realised something profound, not about *her,* but about *me.*

I was *literally* the mother she never had.

I had never considered myself parent material. Even though I didn't know about the abuse, I knew I was too fucked up to ever bring children into the world. And I suspected the world was too fucked up to impose on an innocent child.

(I now disagree with the former, and while I still agree with the latter, I think it's still worth bringing children into the world if you can offer them the care, nurture and unconditional love they deserve).

But it dawned on me. As I grew in confidence in my independence, in my adulthood, and—critically—in my womanhood, the mothering instinct came to the fore.

That changed *everything.*

Suddenly, Little Georgia and I were talking *regularly.* Constantly, even.

She became that happy, chatty child who tugs at your sleeves and wants to show you things. Who wants to know how the world works. Who wants to stop and look at a spider or a pretty flower, just *because.*

I had created an avatar for a creative project that I called Peach Sundae. A delightful little kid in orange dungaree shorts, a yellow sweater and the cutest pigtails.

Little Georgia recognised herself. And adopted 'Peach' as a nickname, and that avatar as her visual representation.

She was really starting to thrive.

And gain confidence.

And for the first time in my life, I *allowed it.*

And *also* for the first time there was no miserable fucker in the way to stop me.

I created a visualisation where Emily is studying hard, concentrating, busy. And Peach is there, looking sad, lonely and distressed. She's tugging on Emily's sleeve for attention, but not getting any.

I invited Emily to step back. To relax. The protective 'front' wasn't necessary any more.

The next visualisation has Emily slouched on a sofa, sipping a can of soft drink through a straw, with a relaxed, content look on her face.

On the floor is Peach. And paper. And paints. And plushies. And a ukulele. Creative chaos, essentially. Peach is joyfully painting, in her own little world. Safe in the knowledge that she's loved, that she's protected, that she can freely express herself without the threat of harm. Or being told she's 'too much'.

The spark is well and truly alive.

Peach is the joy they never touched. The birthright of every six-year-old to be at once fun, joyful, chaotic, naughty.

She's cheeky. She's inappropriate, and does, indeed, require some gentle parenting sometimes — like when she gave me the intrusive thought to start a food fight over lunch at the high-end spa.

I don't berate her. I don't repress her. But I do sometimes suggest that while I *love* her idea, it might be nice if we *don't* get kicked out of the spa, and we *do* get to enjoy the rest of our afternoon there.

As I got in touch with Peach, I started to notice the 'Peach' in others. Especially creatives.

And even more so with comedians.

Watch any comedy sketch show, and you are essentially looking at a bunch of chaotic children playing. They might let their adult selves filter or edit their output. But the spark? That is the inner child. That is *their* 'Peach'. 100%.

I climb once a week with my best friend. Indoor bouldering. And over the course of my abuse discovery and parts-emergence, it has been *incredibly* hit-and-miss.

Bouldering requires physical strength, yes. But also mental aptitude, to figure out how to *actually* get to the top of the climbs. And, more importantly, it requires *emotional strength.*

Catch me on a bad emotional day and I can lose two grades of ability. Honestly. It's not even funny.

I can be half-way up a simple climb and my 'courage meter' suddenly drops to zero and I have to come straight off the wall, tentatively picking my way down a climb that—only moments before—I had been climbing confidently.

The converse is true, though. If you're in good form, *especially* emotionally, you can be *on fire.* You climb confidently. You get to the top of climbs you've been working on for weeks, and it looks like there was never a time when you couldn't do them.

That's what happened to me one day when I woke up feeling vigilant. I never really know who will be at the front when I wake up, and what kind of mood that might put me in.

But on this particular day, it was very much Vanessa and Emily. Vigilance, deportment, correctness, repression... all the things that make for a frankly *awful* climb.

But something clicked in me. I was still lying in bed and I spoke to Vanessa and Emily.

"Girls... why don't you take the day off. Honestly, you've earned it."

And what do you know, they listened. And agreed.

And they plonked themselves on the sofa with cake and soft drinks.

And so Peach grabbed her climbing shoes and chalk and off we went to the wall.

My best friend noticed instantly. I was full of joy. Full of life. We passed the heritage railway on our walk to the wall and a steam train came past.

"OMG!!! TRAINS!!!"

I cried with joy. Like, *actually* began crying. Because of a fucking *train.*

We continued to the wall. We chatted and laughed and maybe even skipped a little on the way.

While we were there I climbed like I hadn't climbed in *months.* I honestly thought I had completely lost my ability to climb over the previous few months while I was sleep-deprived, and with flashbacks echoing in my mind as I tried to scale the wall.

But no. The ability hadn't *gone,* it was merely *buried* under all the crap.

It only took Peach coming to the front to unlock it all.

I said to my friend "Oh my god, imagine what would be possible if Peach was fronting all the time."

I mean, I'd be exhausted, but *apart* from that? The energy. The confidence. The pure contagious joy? Yes, please.

I even let her cheeky chaos-goblin side come out...

We'd been struggling on a climb that was a grade harder than our usual ones. It was one of those where you kinda say "I *know* I can get that... but I just can't get it..." They're the best sort. They keep you coming back.

Well, anyway, another climber saw us struggling. He's much stronger than us. He asked if he could offer some advice, and we said "go ahead".

So he showed us a method to complete the climb that was smooth, and easy — and only needed us to be about three times stronger than we actually are.

I felt the insecurity starting to loom, but Peach piped up, and I didn't stop her...

"Oh wow," she said, "Thank you for showing us a much harder way to do that climb we were struggling with..."

Yep. That's my girl. That's Peach.

No shame. No filter. No apology.

And I fucking love her for it.

She's not mean. She just doesn't stand by while a random guy is flexing in front of a pair of struggling girls.

Good girl, Peach, you little star!

# 24. Safety

Safety is *key* to trauma recovery.

You can't fix the boat while it's still being battered by the storm. You have to find a safe harbour where you can moor up and assess the damage.

Physical safety is a given.

That can include moving *out* of an abusive environment, or *from* a location that abusers know about.

It also includes making sure you have resources — food, shelter, medicine. All the things you need to survive.

I say it's a given. I mean that it's *vital* if a someone is going to become a survivor rather than remaining as a victim. I don't mean it's *easy* or *automatic*.

Getting away can honestly be one of the hardest parts of survival. And if a victim is in a truly dangerous situation, they may have to plan meticulously around their abusers' movements and schedule, and enlist the help of friends or authorities to complete their plan.

I've read reports telling of survivors stocking up the cupboards with groceries the day before their escape to maintain the illusion of the 'happy family'. Then kissing their abuser goodbye, and as he turns left out of the driveway to go to work, their backup team comes in from the right.

Honestly, the precision required is sometimes of a military standard.

But there is truly nothing more heart-warming on the survivors' group than when someone who has previously said "I need to get out" finally makes a post "I made it. I'm in the shelter."

Thank. Fuck.

Another *key* form of safety is *relational* safety.

While physical safety *gets you out,* it's relational safety that *brings you home.*

I had to learn very quickly what relational safety looked like, because I was supporting survivors—my dissociated parts, my girls—as they emerged. But what I learnt would also apply to someone supporting a survivor in their life.

The most important thing is that if my parts didn't feel safe, they wouldn't show themselves. And they wouldn't talk. And they wouldn't *heal.*

One of the first things I learnt was to sit quietly and let them come to me.

I'd actually learnt this lesson many years ago when I was a photographer. I had gone to the local deer park before dawn to get photos of the wildlife with the sunrise. I was a little early, so I sat quietly on a bench and waited.

Wouldn't you know? As I sat there, a small group of deer began to walk over. Tentatively, yes. But approaching all the same.

I sat as still as I could and slowly the deer came right up to me for a sniff. To see what I was all about.

And the moment I moved? They were startled. They ran.

If I'd chased them? If I'd moved towards them at *any time?* They would have been gone in an instant. Deep into the woodland. Nobody would likely see them for the rest of the morning.

I realised that dissociated parts are exactly the same.

**Sit quietly and *let them come.***

Don't force. Don't bombard them with questions. Let them tell you in their own time.

This is *exactly* how you deal with a survivor too.

What else can you do?

**Believe them.**

Oh my god. I've talked about doubt extensively. A survivor has already been through *all* of the doubt. They've thought of *every possible way* to make the abuse not true.

They do *not* need someone to say 'surely not?'

They do *not* need someone to say 'do you think maybe you're mistaken?'

And they don't need someone to say 'that doesn't add up...'

No. Trauma memory is messy. It's fragmented. It takes time for the dots to join up. For the jigsaw pieces to slot into place. Heck, you tend to only get fifty percent of the jigsaw pieces in the first place.

But belief? That is heaven to a survivor.

The most *common* way to greet a new member on the survivors' group is with a simple: I see you. I believe you.

After weeks, months or years of doubting themselves, being gaslit by abusers, and disbelieved by friends, families or authorities, to have someone—*anyone*—say "I believe you" is truly a gift.

❧

It can be tempting to try to *fix* a survivor. Or maybe to fix their *situation.*

But that's not what a survivor needs.

Again, I learnt this with my girls:

***Witness* them, don't *fix* them.**

Simply being *present* for a survivor is, again, a huge gift. Even when things get messy. When they get emotional. When there's silence because they just don't know how to describe the complex feelings inside.

You simply sit with them. No pity. No shame. Just *witness.*

One of the greatest gifts I have *ever* received in my life was the gift of *witness.*

My best friend invited me for a night away. Interesting historic town, nice hotel.

It was the first time I would be sharing a room with anyone since my abuse emerged — and critically, since my flashbacks started.

I'd had one solo trip to a hotel in the meantime and it was hell. Laura was, as you can imagine, *highly* triggered and spent the night re-enacting the abuse, hiding under the bed in terror, and altogether making a most uncomfortable trip.

So I was a little worried. I warned my friend that I *might* have a flashback. Or two. And she said that was okay.

I said I would put together some guidance[22] for her since flashbacks are pretty intense to *experience,* I can't imagine what they're like to *witness.*

So we went away. She had asked for a twin room, but we got a double. That was fine. Except... I was feeling pretty vulnerable. I reiterated the guidelines. Things like "don't worry, I know I'm safe" and "you don't need to *do* anything" and "please feel free to get up, walk about, make a drink, leave the room... you are not abandoning me."

Well... if I didn't have *three* fucking flashbacks that trip. One in the afternoon almost as soon as we arrived, and two overnight.

And they were pretty intense too. The works. Screaming, sobbing, body re-enactments.

---

22 You can read the guidance I prepared at: https://thegirlwhowasthere.com/flashback-guidance

And my friend? She sat there quietly and witnessed me. Through *all* of it.

When I was back in the room, I could see it had affected her. How could it not? I could see the tears welling in her eyes.

But she was a real star. And I let her know that.

Honestly, to have someone else witness such an intense and vulnerable experience is—I don't know—it's intimate. It's validating. It's love. It makes you feel less alone.

And now when she turns up to go climbing and I say "I've had two flashbacks this morning", she knows.

Oh, she knows.

Another *hugely* important thing to survivors is *boundaries.*

The number-one priority of a survivor is to protect their nervous system and protect their peace. They have a *way* different outlook of relationships than non-survivors.

To help a survivor, you can:

**Celebrate their boundaries.**

One definition of love is *knowing that your 'no' is as welcome as your 'yes'*. And survivors need to say 'no' a lot.

Again, this works so well with my own support for my thirty-one girls.

There have been *so many times* over the last eight months that I've *wanted* to go out to my acoustic night, but at least one of my girls has said 'no'.

I'm always disappointed, but they come first. Always.

In these situations, I always say to myself "I'd love to go, but my girls need me."

And I'm not lying.

That's *exactly* why I'm not going. And I don't do it with resentment — I do it with love.

When my girls need me, they need me. Non-negotiable.

So when a survivor sets a boundary—when they say 'no'—they're not being rude. They're not being difficult. They are *literally saving their own life.*

Their rejections—the people they let go of, the events they turn down, the opportunities they pass up—may seem wholly illogical and stupid to a non-survivor. But there are *always* good reasons, even if the survivor can't express them.

A survivor's nervous system is on high alert permanently. In any given moment, it's doing at least a hundred times more work than that of a non-survivor. And because of that, they *have to* protect it the best they can. Anyone who makes them feel unsafe or unseen is likely to be discarded.

Any event—no matter how much they enjoy it—will, if it costs too much nervous energy, be turned down.

Incidentally, if you are still in the life of a survivor who has done a significant amount of healing, then give yourself a pat on the back — their continued friendship is a real testimony to your character.

Another vital way you can help a survivor—and a survivor can help themselves—is to:

**Respect their pace.**

Abuse, especially long-term ritual abuse—is not something you 'just move on' from. Recovery is not linear, not logical and it certainly doesn't adhere to anyone's idea of a timeline.

"When will I be better?" is the question.

The answer? "When you're better."

You can't impose deadlines on recovery. You can't cajole or encourage. You can't set goals — well, you can *try* to set goals if you like, but don't be disappointed if they all go out of the window in an instant.

The pace isn't constant either. Sometimes progress will happen at break-neck speed, sometimes things will seem stuck for days, weeks, months, even years.

There is *nothing* you can do to change the pace, and *attempting* to do so only causes distress.

There are honestly so many ways to be a safe supporter to a survivor and there isn't space here to cover it all.

So the keystone, really, is:

**Ask them what they need — not what happened.**

They *might* want to share details of their abuse. They might not. That's up to them. But they will almost always *need* something. That might be to go out and buy ice cream. It might be to go over the part they don't believe again. Or it might be simply to be left alone, or kept company in silence.

An abuse survivor has suffered huge violations to their autonomy, so putting the control back in *their* hands is empowering and liberating.

I mean, take of the first part of that advice—***ask them what they need***—and you have advice for *all* relationships.

It's pretty simple, yet so seldom followed.

You may find—as in my own experience—that safety is something that a survivor has *never* had in their life.

This was brought home to me in the most vivid way one day mid-way through my discovery of my parts.

I decided I needed a break. Well... to be more accurate, my *therapist* decided I needed a break. She has *never* directed me to do anything, preferring to listen, to accept, and to trust that I know what I need if I'll just get out of my own way.

But this was different. She said it out loud. For the first time ever, she gave me an instruction. "Take some time off."

Not off work, not off chores... off the trauma processing.

And she was right. I *did* need the break.

So one day I decided to set up the ultimate treat for myself. For Peach, really.

I don't have a TV, but I brought my big computer monitor downstairs into the living room and set it up on the coffee table. I cued up a movie—*'My Neighbour Totoro'* from Japan's Studio Ghibli. I swear it's one of the best movies ever made where nothing really happens. If you know it, you'll know what I mean.

I built a nest of blankets and plushies on the sofa.

I made a cup of tea. And a sandwich (cheese and piccalilli — peak grounding survivor food). And I put a couple of chocolate biscuits on the side of the plate.

I pressed play on the movie. Settled in to my nest. And I began sobbing quietly.

Then loudly.

Then bawling — an absolute dam-burst of emotion.

Honestly, it was the *first time in my life* anyone had done something so nice for me. So soft. So *safe*.

I didn't know what to do with it.

That idea of feeling safe? It *completely* overwhelmed me.

I know.

That told me so much.

When I'm doubting whether it was all real, this is one of those touch-points I can rely on. You don't have a full dam-burst of emotion over some blankets and a movie that hasn't even properly started yet, unless some bad stuff happened in your past, and this was the first time you truly felt like it didn't always have to be that way.

Safety, I've learned, isn't something you wait for — it's something you *build.*

Brick by brick. Choice by choice. Boundary by boundary.

Sometimes it's as small as a plushie, sometimes as powerful as a well-placed 'no'. Sometimes as earth-shattering as a movie and a blanket nest.

I never knew what safety felt like before.

But I do now.

And that changes *everything.*

# 25. Saoirse

"I'm so glad I held out..."

I was walking out of the *fifth* shop on a quest for some suitable hair dye.

It all started over lunch. I'd been climbing with my best friend. We'd had our re-fuelling meal, and I asked "do you think it's about time I dyed my hair again?"

She agreed it might be a good idea.

"Mind if I pop into Boots on the way home?" It sounded like a simple side-quest, nothing too involved.

On the way to Boots I was wondering what colour I'd get. Would I go for the safe Light Ash Brown (just writing the name feels like shrinking) or the radiant, fiery Amber that I'd tried last time and actually quite liked.

I was mostly undecided, but by the time we got to Boots, I had pretty much settled on Amber. I deserve to shine. I deserve to be radiant. I don't have to shrink any more.

Long story short, Boots didn't have any. Nor Superdrug. Nor two more shops we tried.

As we entered the fourth shop I said "If they *don't* have Amber, but *do* have Light Ash Brown, I'll take it..."

I knew I was lying.

We entered the fourth shop, and sure enough they had Light Ash Brown, and no Amber.

My lie revealed itself. I really wasn't going to settle.

Having realised that I *deserve* Amber, it was now that or nothing. I would hold out.

And thank goodness I did. We figured out *one more shop* that might stock the dye. Took a bit of a detour to go there. And—cue the choir and heavenly light shining on the hair dye shelf—there was the Amber.

This is Saoirse to a tee.

[It's pronounced *seer'-shuh*, by the way, if you're like me and read out loud in your head]

❧

Saoirse is a lot like Peach. She didn't split off to endure torture. Although what she went through was a kind of slow, mild, infernal soul-crushing torture...

She split off when I changed schools. I was eleven.

My parents had divorced by now. That was good because it meant the bulk of the abuse stopped. But my mother refused financial aid from my father, and refused to make him fund the house we were living in. Knowing what I know now about his financially controlling nature, that was probably a smart move on her part.

We went from being one of the wealthiest families in a mostly middle class street—thanks in part to Laura's efforts, ugh—to poverty. I'm talking real boiled-potatoes-for-dinner-again type poverty.

But at the same time, I won a free place to a private school — smart girl!

I had the academic credentials, but damn, that place was a shock to the system. A *massive* shock.

Despite previously being relatively wealthy, I had never socialised with any wealthy kids. To be fair I hadn't socialised with many other kids at all, Emily was too busy keeping me distant and safe from scrutiny.

But also, the wealth was gone. I remember a classmate, purse open, looking at a five-pound note and saying "oh drat, I'm out of money." I hadn't *seen* a five-pound note for months.

With the move, I lost my old classmates and my sense of connection to everything that had fed my soul. I was put in a harsh environment of competition (which didn't interest me) and status (of which I had none, being broke).

I was there for five years and I ended up completely isolated unable to socialise or relate to my classmates in any way. Even when I left that school and returned to the old system, and even ended up back with some of the girls I'd previously been at school with, I never really connected again... the damage was done. It wasn't until university that I really managed to re-connect and get a much-needed girlie gang back around me.

There's actually a little more to this story, but that's for another book and another time.

So like I said, Saoirse was very much like Peach. She didn't split to protect *me,* like most of my other parts had. The split was to protect *her.* I packaged her up for safety.

I was in an environment that left *no room* for her. No room for softness, for being a princess, for being creative or artistic, for being allowed to dream.

Even after all the abuse I'd suffered, I had a little soul left, and that school did its best to erase it.

I was having none of it.

Just as I had done with Peach six years prior, I took Saoirse and her love of beauty and whimsy, and I packaged her up as tightly as I could. Bubble wrap. Packing paper. Polystyrene peanuts. Anything to keep her *hidden* and *safe* from that hostile, alien environment.

And I got on with gaining my grades. And became *excellent* at over-achieving. Pleasing my teachers. Largely ignoring my peers. And learning the *hustle* that would carry me through a *huge* portion of my adult life.

❧

But the timing of Saoirse's emergence was odd.

Parts that turn up later *tend* to carry significantly worse pain than those who turn up earlier. It takes them longer to trust their 'host', to feel safe, to feel that their story will be met with love and acceptance.

So why did Saoirse wait until twenty-nine other parts had surfaced before she emerged?

Why did she remain buried for *decades?*

The reason?

Basically, she just didn't have *permission* to show herself.

She honestly tried in my twenties. But I was still well within the influence of my mother. Any attempts I made at softness or creativity or, indeed, *joy* were met with ridicule or scorn.

Hell, my mother took me aside one day and told me she and her husband didn't like me having a pink phone cover. I am not making this up.

Instead of seeking and savouring beauty, I leaned into pain.

As I've mentioned before, I got caught up in the BDSM scene. I went to some dark places — literally and figuratively.

Instead of exploring whimsy, I was reaping the punishment I believed I deserved for existing.

Instead of radiating, I was shrinking. Hiding in black jeans, boxy t-shirts and baggy jumpers.

I'd had a foray into being radiant in my twenties but it was short-lived and full of shame. So I shrank again.

It was always about shrinking.

Saoirse carried profound grief and shame. I think that's why she hid for so long.

When she emerged, she really threw me for a loop.

I don't know — she seemed so *insignificant,* so *quiet,* yet was beginning to alter my life beyond recognition.

I distinctly remember waking up one morning. It was mid-October. I tentatively opened the curtains to see what kind of day it might be, and Peach was *straight* in there:

## WOOOO!!! FOG!!!

It was the first foggy day of the year. Not even a light mist, but one of those proper autumnal fogs that at once bring wonder and delight, but also make driving a real hazard.

I walked down to my local shops and this is where Saoirse showed herself. It stopped her dead in her tracks...

A simple spider's web on a bush. Beautifully formed. And with dew drops hanging from the strands like little jewels.

Oh my! She was awe-struck. Mystified. Overwhelmed.

We stood there studying it for the longest time. We thought about the hard-working little spider that had created it. And we thought about the amazing acts of nature and *physics* that had adorned it so beautifully.

That is Saoirse. Stopping to take in the beauty that a busy life has no time or space for.

Where Peach is full of chaos and untamed joy, Saoirse is full of wonder, whimsy and dreamy softness. Literally *everything* I couldn't carry while I was still in 'survival mode'. While I was guarded. Armoured. Alert. Unsafe.

❧

Even before Saoirse emerged, I'd been looking at, buying and wearing much more whimsical and romantic clothing. Ruffles, frills, all the things my mother would hate. Of course, this *was* Saoirse emerging. Just as my more traumatised parts would re-enact the abuse before they showed themselves fully, Saoirse would 're-enact' being beautiful!

I've learnt to *give myself permission*[23] to love what I love. To have what I want. To wear what the fuck I like. To not care what other people think.

I'd admired Mary Oliver's poem *Wild Geese*[24] for years, but when I read the opening five lines again during this part of my healing, they landed in my chest like a revelation.

In just a few lines, she shattered every rule I'd been taught.

I didn't have to be good. I didn't have to apologise for wanting. I could let the soft animal of my body love what it loves — and that was holy.

❧

So, recently I was scrolling my socials and there was a *beautiful* bridesmaid dress in the adverts. Baby pink. Halter neck with matching back. High-low cut so the front is knee-length and the back trails the floor. Asymmetric even, cut higher on the left knee.

In short, it was exquisite — just *exquisite.*

I clicked on it, partly to see how much it might cost, but partly out of habit — I save images of pretty dresses for inspiration. A kind of Saoirse-led mood board.

Holy crap. It was the last one. It was in my size. It was twenty pounds to clear.

What the actual...? Twenty fucking pounds? Crazy!

---

23 If you ever feel you need 'permission' to do, have or say something, I can recommend a visit to: ineedpermission.com. You're welcome!

24 Honestly, I wanted to quote those lines, but after being sent around the houses—or more accurately the *permissions* departments of various publishers—I gave up seeking clearance to post it. Sorry — your girl ain't got time for that shit. You can easily find it online. It's worth a read. As is "The Journey", also by Mary Oliver

I had a quick think. Where the hell would I *ever* wear this dress? I couldn't think of a *single* situation where it would be appropriate. I couldn't even wear it to a wedding because it would show up the bride.

But twenty quid? *Fuck it!* I bought it.

I thought of *two* places I might wear it. Firstly, to wash the dishes. Well — just to wear it around the house for the sake of it. That is actually okay, you know? And secondly, to visit my therapist. She thought that sounded cool — and sugges-ted another place I might wear it: I could pull on my hiking boots and take a long walk out into the countryside in it.

Did I mention that I love my therapist? I like how she rolls!

I've washed the dishes in it. I haven't been to my therapist or for my hike. Yet.

I realised I wasn't *bad* for buying the dress. I wasn't wrong. I wasn't naughty. I wasn't too much.

I have the right to bring beauty and whimsy into my life. Just like seeing to my girls when they need me, that right is *also* a non-negotiable.

While Peach introduced me to the chaotic, unfiltered six-year-old that I never got to be, Saoirse introduced me to the beautiful, developing young lady — the girl on the brink of womanhood who could have carried softness, love, whimsy and quiet aesthetic joy, but instead had it all taken away from her.

She remained buried and longing for so many years. Literally decades.

But now?

Saoirse, I see you. I love you. You are safe now.

You have permission to come out and express yourself fully.

You never *needed* permission.

But you have it.

# 26. Home

I thought I was done. Thought my healing was 'complete'.

Silly girl! Of course it wasn't — I'm not sure our healing is *ever* truly 'complete.'

My last part—Ruth—had emerged three weeks prior. Such a breath of fresh air after the chaos of the peak. That's when I would go into therapy and say "just four new parts this week..." and think nothing of it. That's the *normalisation* we talked about way back in Chapter Eight.

And flashbacks? The last one I'd logged was eleven days prior. Again, a far cry from the three or four *per day* that I was getting when they were coming thick and fast.

Yeah, this was *definitely* a change.

But then, out of the blue, I found myself re-enacting the abuse again. Dammit. I thought I was done with that.

Of course, now I simply allowed it happen, refused to feel shame, refused to beat myself up further for 'slipping', and simply went about my day.

I recognise that re-enactment isn't regression. It's simply what happens. It's simply part of life for a survivor.

Later that evening, I had pretty much the most intense and epic flashback I'd ever experienced. I'll hand over to the report I wrote afterwards:

*Now that was an experience.*

*It started with sobbing. And a little shaking. A general grief for what happened.*

*And then Rachel showed up and we grieved, then Claire... then Laura...*

*One by one each girl showed up... some with intense flashbacks, some more calm... But I don't think a single one of my parts was absent...*

*I don't know how long it went on for... It's about twenty-eight minutes since I was last aware of the time, so maybe it took that long...*

*Wow.*

*This feels like such strong integration... the fact that every single one of my girls can show up in the same grief/flashback episode...*

*Honestly, it was a little difficult to endure, but it has also filled me with joy... like they're all home... They're all here... No one is hiding any more...*

*Truly fascinating. I feel that was a threshold I stepped over tonight... And it feels good...*

*Another step to being healed (whatever that means).*

> *I love my girls so much and I am so proud of myself for how I've handled this whole discovery process since February.*
>
> *Just over eight months now and I feel I've come to a place that many people never achieve. Or take decades to reach if they do.*
>
> *Good girl, Georgia. Your self-love and refusal to abandon yourself has paid off, even if it hurt so badly at the time.*
>
> *Well done, I'm proud of you.*

The difference is palpable, right? You see it, don't you?

Flashbacks no longer bring the chaos they used to. Or the distress. Or the shame.

This one? Filled with safety. Trust. *Sovereignty.*

I wasn't hijacked. I didn't suffer. I didn't second-guess.

I simply allowed it to flow through me.

*Allowed it.*

I think that's really the key to healing.

We might *never* be free of the flashbacks or the re-enactments or the memories or the grief, but healing represents a change in our *relationship* with what happened, and with what continues to show up.

I may well still have hidden parts — exiled girls carrying things even heavier than those I've already met. I certainly still have unanswered questions, so I wouldn't be surprised.

But, importantly, I'm not afraid of them any more.

I trust myself now. I trust myself to meet whatever comes — with compassion, with boundaries, and with truth. That's what healing gave me — not perfection or resolution, but the unshakeable sense that whatever happens next, *I've got me. And I've got my girls.*

I think that is the true goal here — integration. It's not about being 'fixed', it's about being 'whole.'

❧

The flashback that night made one thing clear: *the girls are home now.*

Not buried. Not in exile. Not trapped in isolated fragments of memory.

They're here, with me, in this life — in the climbing gym, on the keyboard, in my bed at night, in the decisions I make every single day.

Integration doesn't mean they disappeared.

It means they no longer have to hide.

And honestly? I'd miss them now if they did disappear. I've come to know them so well, to love them, to listen to them. They're not just memories — they're *family.*

There's no single moment where integration happens, no fireworks or finish line. No certificate to say 'well done!' Just the gradual realisation that no part of me is being left behind any more.

That's what home means.

That's what healing gave us.

I think if you ask any survivor what they wish for, it would be freedom — freedom from pain and shame, from the past, from the flashbacks.

It's easy to wish that none of it had happened. But wishes like that don't come true.

Instead, we have to find freedom in a new form.

We learn to *live with* the flashbacks. Sometimes they're intense; sometimes they hover in the background, quietly gnawing away. Sometimes they make you cry in the toilets of the climbing gym, which is *exactly* what happened on the morning I wrote these closing words.

Our freedom doesn't come from forgetting our history, but who we become *because* of it.

I've become a fierce, relentless advocate for *myself* — for my safety, for my peace.

I've learnt radical self-acceptance.

I've learnt to release shame, blame and guilt, and to direct anger where it belongs: on the shoulders of those who hurt and violated me.

But most of all? I have learnt to unapologetically and relentlessly love myself and *all* of my girls. All thirty-one of them.

**Freedom isn't the absence of pain, it's the presence of love.**

**To My Girls...**

**Vanessa, Emily** — Thank you for carrying so much for me, for protecting me and looking after the the other girls. You can rest now.

**Rachel, Clare, Zoe, Rebecca, Kat, Amanda, Olivia** — I am *so* sorry you had to endure what you did. You are safe now.

**Laura, Joanna, Allie, Jane, Julia, Andrea, Annabelle** — I see what they did to you. You never have to forgive them if you don't want to. You are home now.

**Debbie, Fiona, Melanie, Holly** — What happened to you was outrageous. No child should have to go through that. I am so sorry. You are safe now.

**Eve, Melissa, Sarah, Ruth** — Please don't feel guilty. Nothing that happened was your fault. The shame and blame falls *squarely* on the shoulders of those who programmed and coerced you. You are safe now.

**Samantha, Katie, Louise, Charlotte** — I know you think you should have done something differently, done something to stop it, but if you could you would. None of this was your fault. You are blameless now. (You always were)

**Peach, Saoirse** — Please don't change. Please keep being *exactly* who you are. The world is better off for you being in it! You are free now.

...and **Chloe** — You were *always* wanted. You were *always* loved. You will never be abandoned again. I'm here now.

*I love you all so, so much.*

**Welcome Home.**

Printed in Dunstable, United Kingdom

72287066R00163